What We Can Learn from the East

∞∞

BEATRICE BRUTEAU

Crossroad • New York

Chapter VI, "Gospel Zen," first appeared
in *Living Prayer*, July-August, 1989.

Chapter VII, "The Immaculate Conception,
Our Original Face," was first published
in *Cross Currents*, Vol. XXXIX, #2, Summer, 1989.

1995
The Crossroad Publishing Company
370 Lexington Avenue, New York, NY 10017

Printed in the United States of America

Library of Congress Cataloging-in-Publication Data

Bruteau, Beatrice, 1930–
    What we can learn from the East / Beatrice Bruteau.
        p.   cm.
    Includes bibliographical references.
    ISBN 0-8245-1457-2 (pbk.)
    1. Christianity and other religions. 2. East and West.
    3. Experience (Religion). I. Title.
    BR128.A77B78   1995
    261.2—dc20   94-46868
                                                    CIP

Contents

Introduction

T HE RECENT Parliament of the World's Religions has confirmed and further energized the interest of the religions
in one another. Thousands of people, representing hundreds
of religious bodies, gathered in Calcutta and Chicago in the
summer of 1993 to share their wisdom and to celebrate their
unity in variety. Christians in particular are showing increas-
ing eagerness to become acquainted with spiritual traditions
adjacent to their own. What may have looked like a tempo-
rary fad in the sixties seems to be settling into a mainstream
and regular area of learning and practice.

Our planetary world has become so accessible, we are so
much in touch with one another now, that hardly anything is
truly "exotic," outside the realm of "our" life. Everything is
coming *inside*. Others aren't nearly so "other" as they once
were. They are much more like variants on the basic human
theme, therefore neighbors and fellow travellers, whose vari-
ations we need not feel as threats but can regard with friend-
ly interest, even sympathy. As often happens when we get to
know people, they turn out to be not so strange after all. In
the case of the world's religions, we have reached the stage
of entering one another's kitchens, swapping recipes, and
sharing confidences over a cup of coffee. We are starting seriously to learn from one another.

The present volume was occasioned by an organization called Retreats International asking to have someone talk to them about what they might learn from Eastern spiritual traditions. These people (Lutherans, Episcopalians, Roman Catholics, and others) are themselves spiritual guides and directors of retreats. Their request was motivated not only by personal openness but also by the hope that they would be stimulated to fresh insights that they could take to their retreat work. My feeling on receiving the invitation was that this was a sign that the spiritual heritage of India and the Far East is neither off-limits nor a curiosity, but is closer to being a routine resource.

More and more departments of religion in colleges are including the wisdom traditions of the whole world as regular offerings in their curriculums. Many people are doing cross-traditional studies, and there is beginning to develop a conversational space in which allusions can be made to various classical lineages in support of some particular point a speaker is making. We are beginning to experience some degree of integrality as we assimilate selected items from the rich board spread before us. By the time the received nourishment has actually passed into our own being, into our life and spirit, it is not a medley of conflicting ideas and practices. If we are able so to sustain a unified life with satisfaction and continued positive aspiration and energized creativity, then we demonstrate that we are moving into a new era in which we can legitimately draw from the spiritual resources of any tradition of the world that appeals to us and can find a *living* way to *incorporate* it into our own actual being. It is insight into this possibility that I hope the reader will gain from these little pieces.

Besides the series prepared for Retreats International, I have included here two essays that tend to the same end: "Gospel Zen" [originally published in *Living Prayer*] suggests that the Gospel can be read as instructions for meditation practices; and "The Immaculate Conception, Our

Original Face" [from *Cross Currents*] proposes that both West and East have icons for the same spiritual discovery of our ground-reality. Typical reaction to these has been, first, that Christians are delighted to find that another tradition can say things so helpful to them, and second, that moving around a little inside the other tradition can suddenly enable them to see a new line of interpretation for very familiar materials. What had been projected outside onto a single heroic figure may now be seen as a revelation of one's own inner life, and thus one may be encouraged to search through the whole body of one's own received wisdom to see if there are other instances in which the new angle of interpretation can be applied.

This is, of course, the effect that any author/teacher most hopes for. A clue gained from thus "traveling abroad" may open the "family Bible" in such a way that one can read there about areas and dimensions of the spiritual life that one supposed were not treated in those texts; but now that we know better what to look for, we are able easily to find it.

A last advantage that one may enjoy from hearing two or three spiritual traditions conversing with each other is a kind of revitalization of one's own interest in religion and spirituality. If one's faith has become too familiar, too flat, too routine, this may spark it afresh. If it has become too irrelevant, too incredible, too naïve, this may reveal its hidden depths and truer meanings, its capacities to challenge and to speak meaningfully to our time and place.

This is the sort of thing that constantly happens to me as I try to bring into my inner conversation speakers from various areas—not only the great mystical religions but also science and even business. I find it very exciting, with new vistas opening up, with creativity burgeoning from this vigorous interaction, and with no end in sight. I believe that this is the wave of our immediate future and that we can ride it with confidence and elation.

Religion Is Experience

THE FIRST THING we can learn about religion from the East is that it is a matter of direct experience. "If God is real, God can be realized" was a favorite saying of Swami Vivekananda. Buddhists wouldn't say "God," of course, but they would agree that the whole thing is a matter of experience, not of theory. (The word "experience" is used here to indicate the most general state or activity of consciousness; it must be understood not to imply the presence of an object that is *experienced by* a subject.) An Easterner tends not to ask, as a Westerner would, "What do you believe?" The Easterner wants to know, "What is your experience?" Even an apparently theoretical question, like "Why did Bodhidharma come from the West?" or "What is Buddha-nature?" or "What is Ultimate Reality?" is answered by plunging both questioner and answerer into immediate experiential reality, not by expounding a theory or citing an item of a creed.

A Canadian woman who attended the Parliament of Religions held in Calcutta reported that Indians would approach various people whom they took to be "holy people" and ask them about their religious experience, what they had realized, how they had done it; they showed no concern for which religion those "holy people" professed or represented.

If you go to a religious teacher in an Eastern tradition, you don't get instruction in catechism, a set of correct answers to chosen questions. You aren't expected to make a commitment to a list of propositions in theology or to believe that the history of the world has taken a certain course, that certain historical events occurred in the past. You are not expected to accept that the world is organized according to certain authority structures, obedience and loyalty to which is a central religious practice. You may, after some time of mutual observation and assessment, ask the teacher to accept you as a disciple. Then, if accepted, you will get training in certain practices, an exposure to a variety of experiences. It will all be concrete, experiential, pragmatic. The teacher will work with you according to what suits *you*, what works for *you*. The teacher is prepared to train different people in quite different ways. There will be no attempt to make you conform to a pregiven pattern. You will be aided toward realization of God in your own peculiar way, which it is the teacher's job to discern. That is, of course, if you get a good teacher, one who does it right.

The point is that the approach to and the practice of the "religion" are adjusted to the person, not the person to the religion. This is a rather interesting matter for us in the West, for we believe that the religion is given by God in an authoritative form, accurately represented by authorized conceptual systems and forms of words and actions, and that the proper response of the religious individual is to accept these forms and conform to the required beliefs, ideas, attitudes, and behaviors.

What can we learn from this? One possibility is that we might adopt more experiential *means* to bring people into line with the authoritative religion as *end*. Quite a number of people have said that if you *act* in the way that Christianity requires, you will gradually come to *believe*.

Another possibility is that we might look upon the experience as the *end* and the beliefs and behaviors as the *means*. We might make reference to St. Paul's remark that faith will be replaced by knowledge and vision; hope will be replaced by fulfillment and possession; but love will remain love forever.

Another possibility is that we might see better that the practices we do require or recommend are useful for bringing consciousness to God-realization. It may be that we are still doing many of these things simply because they are required to fulfill a duty or obligation, or to avoid a sin, or because they are traditional, or because we are used to doing them and they have become part of our self-image and part of our sense of belonging to our particular tradition. The Eastern teacher would say that those reasons for doing religious practices are not only poor but that some of them are positively injurious—the ones that reinforce separative self-images and group-membership images. But, that teacher would point out, many of these practices are in themselves valuable and can be turned to good account if done with the view that they are to lead to experience of God.

Prayer practices, meditation, service to the poor, recitation of scriptures, worship in the temple, devotional song and dance, repetition of the names of God, adoration directed to God through the mediation of icons—these are some things that are common to both East and West. The difference might be simplistically summarized by saying that in the East these are considered privileges rather than obligations. There isn't, so far as I know, a sense that adoration is *due* God. The feeling I have picked up is that adoration is the delight of the devout soul and aids the devotee in coming closer to realization. In general, there is no sense of a *legal* relation to God, even in the muted sense of a covenantal relation. The relation seems rather to be *natural*. This is why the accent is on the religious *experience*, rather than on fulfillment of commands, obedience, loyalty, belonging to the church, etc.

The Easterner feels that since God-realization is the goal, it is desirable to abandon ideas, feelings, practices that tend to reinforce one's identification with finite characteristics of one's selfhood. A really serious practitioner has to renounce caste and cult, anything that might separate one from God and other people. This is just the opposite of the Western feeling that the important religious act is to belong to and be loyal to a particular community that has separated itself from others, from outsiders and unbelievers. Christians will not practice their religion together with other Christians, even, unless they belong to the proper denominations—in some cases, not even with other individual congregations of the same denomination. And this is not considered by them to be sinful weakness but rather dutiful and especially faithful practice, a proper religious act.

What could be learned from the East, therefore, would be the idea of possibly reassessing this attitude of separation, of communion only with insiders. If the main thing is union with God, the East suggests, then *how* you get there is of secondary importance. When you transfer the importance to the area of *how* and insist that your way alone is correct, then you stray from what is really the prime value and reality. Something that can be learned from the East —which, admittedly, doesn't always practice it, either—is to view other religions not only with tolerance but with genuine respect and acceptance. If the accent is on experience rather than theory, creed, or church membership, then all religions may have a great deal in common although expressed in their diverse ways. When one is in quest of the experience, one becomes willing to learn from all sources, whether or not they are of one's culturally received tradition. And this very attitude of openness, of refusing to practice exclusion, is itself a great help toward preparing for divine experience, the Eastern teacher would say. It loosens the attachment to one's own sense of privileged position in the scheme of things, thus removing one obstacle in the way of realization of the Universal Ground and Ultimate Reality. So what is this God-realization I keep talking about? What *is* the Experience? It is what we call *mystical union.*

The word "mysticism" has been so abused that I think it best to make a point of saying in the beginning what I do not mean by "mysticism." I do not mean parapsychological phenomena, such as extrasensory perception, precognition, retrocognition, mental telepathy, psychometry, out-of-body experiences, or communication with the dead by means of automatism, mediums, or direct visions and voices. I do not mean paraphysical phenomena, such as extramedical healings, auras, concern with etheric or astral bodies, poltergeists, other instances of psychokinesis, levitation, magical influences over persons and circumstances, and miracles. I do not mean occult sciences, such as numerology, alchemy, palmistry, astrology, or magical architecture. I do not mean altered states of consciousness in which one perceives extraordinary colors, shapes, sounds, fragrances, and flavors, or feels transported into other dimensions, or finds his ego dissolved and his body expanded to fill the universe, or discovers that everyone is lovable, and experiences ecstatic joy and delight. I do not mean revelations from saints, angels, deities, or other discarnate entities, who have prophetic messages, warnings, or promises for the world. I do not mean cosmic consciousness, in which one has a vision of the cosmos as a whole, with all its history and meanings displayed and comprehended.

I do not mean religious experiences in which one turns from a life of sin or neglect of God to a life of righteousness and communion with God, or in which one is favored with a sense of the presence of the deity. I do not mean being possessed by one's God, filled with the Holy Spirit, or any other enthusiastic state.

The elimination of these phenomena does not imply that I consider them to be fraudulent or nonsense or otherwise unworthy. They may or may not be. And they differ greatly among themselves, not all being on the same level of respectability by any means. But none of them is quite *mysticism*—although two or three of them approach or resemble that state—and therefore in what I have to say I will not be referring to them.

What, then, is "mysticism"? To be a mystic is to experience absolute Reality, or absolute Being. The Reality is absolute, that is, not relative. Not being relative, it cannot have form, for all forms are relative to one another. Thus, it is infinite. Being infinite or formless, absolute Being will be experienced as transcending space and time, as well as all possible categories of the understanding. Thus, it is invisible, eternal, inconceivable, and unspeakable. It cannot be known either by the senses or by the mind, for both of these modes of conscious experience involve form, either material or conceptual.

And, most important, because the Reality is absolute, to experience it is not to relate to it as subject to object. To know it as object would be to be conscious of it as relative to oneself as knower and one's act of knowing, and this would contradict its nature as absolute and at once invalidate the consciousness. So the consciousness must be one in which the duality of subject and object is transcended. To realize oneself as "one with the One," this is mysticism.

In the *Mandukya Upanishad,* one of the oldest treatises on mysticism, compiled some time before 500 B.C., it is said that mystical consciousness is "beyond the senses, beyond understanding, beyond all expression. . . . It is pure unitary consciousness, wherein awareness of the world and of multiplicity is completely obliterated. It is ineffable peace. It is the supreme good. It is one without a second. It is the Self."

In the fourteenth century of our era, Jan Van Ruysbroeck, a Flemish Christian, said that in the mystical state, one's "spirit is undifferentiated and without distinction, and therefore it feels nothing but the unity."

St. Teresa of Avila, in the sixteenth century, described this unity by saying, "It is like rain falling from the heavens into a river or a spring: there is nothing but water there and it is impossible to divide or separate the water belonging to the river from that which fell from the heavens. Or it is as if a tiny streamlet enters the sea, from which it will find no way of separating itself, or as if in a room there were two large windows through which the light streamed in: it enters in different places but it all becomes one."

The third-century Neoplatonic philosopher Plotinus gives this account: "There are not two; beholder is one with the beheld. It is not a vision compassed but a unity apprehended. . . . This is why the vision baffles telling. We cannot detach the supreme to state it. If we have seen something thus detached, we have failed of the supreme, which is to be known only as one with ourselves."

A ninth-century Chinese Zen monk gives this account of his enlightenment and how he felt afterwards:

> Wherever I went I met words and did not understand them. A lump of doubt inside the mind was like a willow-basket. For three years, residing in the woods by the stream, I was altogether unhappy. Then unexpectedly I happened to meet the Zen master sitting on the rug. I advanced toward him, earnestly asking him to dissolve my doubt. The master rose from the rug on which he sat deeply absorbed in meditation. He then, baring his arm, gave me a blow with his fist on my chest. This all of a sudden exploded my lump of doubt completely to pieces. Raising my head I, for the first time, perceived that the sun was circular. Since then I have been the happiest man in the world, with no fears, no worries. Day in day out, I pass my time in a most lively way. Only I notice my inside is filled with a sense of fullness and satisfaction. I do not go out any longer, hither and thither, with my begging bowl for food.

Richard Rolle likewise says of those who are established in the unitive way: "all their inward parts are glad with pleasant shining light." They "feel gladdened with merriest love, and in joyful song wonderfully melted," for they have drunk the heavenly wine of life, which "fulfills the soul."

St. John of the Cross promises one who is on the mystic way: "indeed very soon, divine calm and peace will be infused into his soul, together with a wondrous and sublime knowledge of God, enclothed in divine love." St. Catherine of Genoa says: "when the soul is naughted and transformed . . . the state of this soul is then a feeling of such utter peace and tranquility that it seems to her . . . in her human and her spiritual nature, both within and without, she can feel no other thing than sweetest peace." And St. Augustine of

Hippo confesses to God, "When I shall cleave to Thee with all my being, then shall I in nothing have pain and labor. And *my life shall be a real life,* being wholly full of Thee."

One of the earliest Zen traditions, composed by the Third Chinese Patriarch in the sixth century, contains these words:

> Should you desire immediate correspondence with reality, all
> that can be said is "No duality!" When there is no duality, all
> things are one, there is nothing that is not included. The
> enlightened of all times and places have all entered into this
> truth.

And in our own times we have people like Margaret Noble, the Irish disciple of Swami Vivekananda, who, as Sister Nivedita, played a prominent role in India's struggle for independence. Her biographer describes her state of mind toward the end of her life, saying, "The all-powerful idols worshiped in the secret of the heart . . . are all thrown one day away because form has lost its meaning. . . . She had become at once the source and the ocean, and all that passes from one to the other."

Simone Weil, a French Jew attracted to Christianity, who had a great sensitivity to the plight of the poor and the need for social reform, expressed her grasp of reality by saying, "God can only be present in creation under the form of absence. . . . This world, insofar as it is completely empty of God is God Himself. . . . That is the mystery of mysteries. When we touch it we are safe."

Thomas Merton, noted monk and writer, attracted to Zen Buddhism, testified from his own experience that contemplatives of both traditions seek "to penetrate the ground of being and of knowledge . . . by the purification and expansion of the moral and religious consciousness until it reaches a state of super-consciousness or meta-consciousness-realization in which subject and object become one."

Now, if this is truly the goal of life, the end of religion, then when we guide retreats or counsel people in spiritual direction, we can securely take the attitude that *this* is the point of all that we are recommending or pointing to. We can resolve never to lose sight of this one goal, the only thing that is truly *necessary*, and not wander off into merely psychological advice on how to get along in daily worldly life. In particular, we can take pains to avoid *using* religion as a means to improve worldly life, to help us "cope." I'm afraid a great many people have the idea, consciously or unconsciously, that religion exists to help them get through life, and they apply to God and to the saints for all sorts of assistance, relief, and advantage. I wouldn't want to say that we ought never to pray for any of these things, but I would stress that we take care not to let our priorities, our sense of means and ends, become inverted. God-realization is the only thing that matters, and everything else is to be ordered to *that*. I would urge that one of the things we can either learn from or be supported in by the East is that we ought constantly to hold this ideal before ourselves and those with whom we discuss these matters. Transcend psychology for religion and religion for spirituality and realization.

Of course, we all develop through stages. One way of describing one lineup of stages is by means of the *chakras*, the "wheels" or "centers of consciousness" through which the energy of manifestation in the finite order ascends to reunion with the Infinite of which it is, so to speak, the "flip side." The energy, in the Hindu tradition, is called *Shakti* and the Infinite is called *Shiva*. The union is spoken of as a marriage. We might compare the relation of the Father and the Son, who indwell one another, the Son being the "exegete" or manifestation of the invisible Father (John 1:18). The centers of consciousness can be identified as security, pleasure, power, love, creativity, insight, and divine union. Let me give an example of how we might use an Eastern teaching to elucidate a Christian story.

I call my interpreted version of this story "The Seven Husbands of the Samaritan Woman."[1] I see it, in a way, as a *koan*, a "case," a mythicized account of an exchange between

two or more people in the context of the quest for enlightenment. The people may not be just people but may verge on
being archetypes, and the relation between them or the com-
bination of them may be the symbol for, or the provocation
to see, something important. Also, the *account* of what
passed between them may be read on several levels. In this
context, which is a Zen context, I see this conversation
between Jesus and the Samaritan woman as *dharma* combat.

When Zen practitioners have had deep experiences of
enlightenment but wish to be tested and to go deeper still,
they seek meetings with other advanced practitioners or
masters. What they say to one another on these occasions
[for instance, "Why did Bodhidharma come from the West?"
"The oak tree in the front garden"] does not make sense to
someone who is not "in on" the code [translation: "What is
Buddha-nature, the Ultimate Reality?" "Everything, in all its
local particularity, is Buddha-nature"], the multilayered
meanings of their apparently simple remarks, as they alter-
nately challenge and respond to one another.[2]

Drawing on the Hindu tradition, I interpret the conversation and particularly the "husbands" in terms of the *chakras*,
or centers of consciousness, and the union of *Shiva* and *Shakti*.
I read the interchange from both sides, as the woman meeting
the guru at the point when she is ready, and as Jesus meeting
his Sophia in order to bring up his full consciousness, a kind
of follow-through on his baptismal experience. I note that the
story begins by saying that Jesus "had to pass through"
Samaria and closes with both Jesus and the woman fully satisfied through what they have exchanged with each other.

The story gets underway when Jesus comes to the Well,
the "deep" Well, given by "our father Jacob," who was sur-
named "Israel"—the one who had struggled with God and
won through to a new identity. Jesus is said to be "tired." He
rests beside the Well, and his disciples go into town to buy
food. He is left alone. Now the Woman comes. She also is

alone, and the hour is noon. High Noon, hour of combat, of confrontation.

Jesus opens by saying, "Give me a drink" (John 4:7). She counters with another question: "How is it that you, a Jewish man, ask drink of me, a Samaritan woman?" Our attention is called to one layer of the symbolic values of the actors. If the Jews claim that they have the true doctrine and that the Samaritans are in error, why this request? Nevertheless, the request has been lodged. She has something to give.

He also has something to give and advances the challenge to the next level: the level of the gift of God, living water, connected with knowledge of the one who asks for drink (4:10): "If you knew the gift of God, and who it is that is saying to you, 'Give me a drink,' you would have asked him and he would have given you living water."

She meets him on this level and points out that the source of water, the Well, is deep, and he has no instrument for drawing (4:11-12). How does he propose to get this living water (and transmit it to her)? "Have you got something better than what this Well supplies?"

I interpret the Well—Jacob's Well—as the traditions of the people, the revelation by which both the Jews and the Samaritans have been living. She understands him immediately as claiming that this revered and revelatory tradition is to be superceded. This is a very daring thought (do we dare to think that way about *our* sacred tradition?), so the conversation has quickly reached a high pitch, a tense moment. Her questions are acting as the "drawing" instrument for him, drawing the water of further revelation up out of him.

He is ready for this question because he knows the source of the Well itself. The Well of tradition does not satisfy; it provokes continuing thirst (which is not a bad thing). But the water he is speaking of comes from an *interior well;* it becomes in one "a fountain of water springing up to eternal life" (4:14). Therefore, mediating instruments for reaching the water are unnecessary: the water comes of its own accord. The source of life is not outside or separate from the living one. The question of replenishment does not arise; the life is eternal.

The Samaritan woman knows exactly what is being said and is ready in her turn: "Give me this water that I may not thirst, nor come here to draw." The giving begins by putting all previous trips to the Well in perspective, lining up her whole quest—"everything she's ever done"—as a clear progress. Let's review and see where you are now: "Call your husband and come" (4:16). What have you been joining yourself to? To what are you wedded now? Her claim of readiness matches his claim of ability to give. She can answer, "I'm not wedded to anything. I'm free and ready to move forward. I claim complete detachment—except for my unfulfilled thirst."

He answers, "This is well said. You have tried—and discarded or moved beyond—five life-mates.[3] You are now engaged with a sixth—but neither is this your true husband." She knows this, of course, as she has just stated and as she has shown by her action of coming again to the Well.

What are these six unions? What does the symbolism mean? It has to be perfectly clear by now that this is not a literal woman and the so-called "husbands" are not, of course, a series of male human beings. The woman is easily—and usefully, for us—interpreted as the questing, thirsting, human soul (mind/heart, consciousness). Her "husbands," then, are the different attitudes she has taken toward life, the goals she has given herself to, the aspects under which she has perceived the reality of the world and the meaning of her existence, the attempts she has made to assuage her "thirst," the series of drawings at the Well of Life that she has made. We might say that these are her answers to such questions as What do I want? What is the most important value? Who am I? She has tried different answers. She has given herself to one view after another, built her life around first this ideal and then that, and discarded or outgrown them one by one. But she hasn't been floundering; she's been growing. Five levels of human aspiration tried but not settled for; a sixth that she is working with but which she is wise enough to know by now is not yet it, so she isn't wedded to it. There is a seventh husband yet to come: this interior spring of eternal life is what she has waited for. What are the stages of life? What are some of the things we "marry" as we go along? Or, what are the assumptions we make about who we are and what we want and what the whole thing is all about? There are, of course, many ways to identify or describe these seven husbands. The way that immediately occurred to me was to liken them to the seven *chakras*. The *chakra* imagery also uses union with the ideal husband as the final goal, the moving energy of embodied consciousness finally merging in the quiescence (eternity, "sabbath rest") of the supreme consciousness. l will run through them briefly here as an example of how we may understand this.

The first husband represents a life-style sometimes spoken of as "living to eat." The dimensions of life are simple direct pleasures and comforts; the goal of life is a good income, a house, a car, the latest appliances, the "good life." When the questing soul realizes that this is insufficient, it divorces itself from this life goal and joins itself to another, somewhat broader and less ego-centered, the first stirrings of the creative impulse.

The second husband refers to sexual energy. This could be stimulating relations with other people, something exciting, something moving and going on and making one feel successful in a fairly local way. For most people this will be raising a family and feeling pride and satisfaction in continuing one's tribe, in reproducing and externalizing and multiplying oneself. However, this may prove to be too small for some souls and they will look farther afield.

The third husband is more ambitious, symbolizing a position and activity of power, a larger scope for one's creativity. This can take the form of a career, of building up an enterprise, of controlling assets or people, a feeling of dominating some kind of a world, even if a relatively small one. The satisfaction here is not in the body or the emotions but more in the mind. But just because it is closer to the spiritual, the soul with a strong questing drive will find that this third marriage induces after a time a sense of malnutrition and has to be forsaken for something quite different, for which nevertheless it has prepared the appetite.

The experience with power and the degree of creativity it involves may generate enough sense of energy in the soul that it can discover that a far more satisfying experience of creativity can be had from a reversal of direction of its driving energies: from self-seeking it is moved to engage in unselfish love for other persons. This is a big jump, a kind of Rubicon-crossing in the journey of the soul, decentering and expanding it. The shift is such a revolution that it makes one feel as though one has at last found the Real Thing, the true meaning of life.

This fourth marriage is deeper and more serious, and the soul gives itself to it more consciously and more thoroughly. Appreciation of the *person* as such appears and grows, concern for the other self in the other's own terms, instead of in terms of how the other can be pleasing or useful to me. The fourth husband doesn't exactly prove unsatisfactory, but what it represents expands.[4] Perhaps one is "widowed" from this level and tenderly handed on to the next level of development.

The fifth husband means creativity with a transcendent, sacred aura. It includes whatever can be experienced as a creative art of high and pure aspiration. One can be truly wedded to one's art, to one's creative work, giving one's whole life to it as a sacred dedication, feeling that one is getting very close to divine life, to a mysterious realm from which that which is greater than oneself passes through oneself and takes body from oneself. Inspiration and beauty and revelation appear and incarnate themselves in creatures of form, color, sound, words, gestures, actions.

Deep living with the fifth husband produces profound satisfactions that are not of this world and enlarges the capacity of the soul for still greater experience, leading to a holy frustration with the limitations of the externalized, or material, world. What one yearns to express can never quite be put into the medium of one's art. Thus one is drawn more and more inward, toward the source of beauty and inspiration and revelation within, toward Absolute Beauty.

The sixth lover—who is still not the true husband—is some version of the contemplative life, in the mind/heart alone, in intellectual intuitions and realizations difficult to express. The old ego-centered self has been dissolving ever since the fourth marriage, gradually forgotten in the greater interest of the larger and more creative worlds. At the sixth level, it has worn away, except for its drive to find the Totally Real, and consciousness has increased to the point where one knows what one knows, what one does not know, cannot know, what is not "knowable," and why. One understands the tricks of attachment and has broken free of them ("I have no husband"). This time, curiously, one knows that this is not yet the end, although one is very close.

By the time she gets to the sixth level of development, she has become fairly sophisticated about what she is doing. She knows quite clearly that she seeks the Absolute—Absolute Being, Goodness, Truth, Beauty; Absolute Consciousness, Absolute Bliss. No *relative* being, goodness, truth, or happiness will answer. Nothing that can be compared to something else or find its meaning by reference to something other than itself. Thus she knows that it has to be sought within herself; all external things are certainly relative. Thus it is also beyond the images put forward by any particular human religion or system of spirituality. (Of course, some of them say of themselves that all their images, all their teachings have to be transcended in the end.) But she also knows, by the same token, that the Absolute Reality/Value is beyond all her own private images, synthesized from all the nourishment she has found in her various experiences and researches. This is why she is not wedded to this one. She also knows that she must be absolutely free from identification of herself in any particular way; you can't continue clinging to certain forms and ideas and ways of doing and still expect to ascend into the heaven of the Absolute. This is why the sixth state is represented as being "alone." All this she knows with crystal clarity. This is why she is represented in the story as appearing at high noon, in the most intense light. What she knows in this light is that what she seeks is necessarily beyond anything that can be known. It has to be a state of *Being.* This is why, when Jesus says that the water they are both thirsty for is a fountain within oneself springing up to eternal life, she knows that he knows, and she proceeds to "draw" it out of him by means of her questions.

Each ascent from level to higher level, imaged here as taking another husband, also represents a trip to the Well, for the soul does all these things watered by the traditions of her people, whatever culture she is living in. Our Samaritan woman, therefore, is a questing soul that is *ready* to pass from the sixth lover to the seventh and true husband.

The "passage" itself is figured as the transcendence of tradition and culture,[5] the interiorization of the Well. The *dharma*-combat continues as the woman puts this question squarely: "How about the traditions of our people?" And Jesus answers, "None of the above" (4:21). This is beyond any culture's particular tradition. You've got to go past the "watchmen of the walls" to find "the one whom [your] soul loves" (Song of Solomon 3:4), past all cultural protections, all means—instruments for "drawing"—and just *be* "in spirit and in truth" (4:24). The woman then throws her final challenge to him—for her, a direct assault on the summit: "How about the 'Messiah,' that is, the final revelation of everything?" And the ultimate revelation, the passage from even the highest intuition to actual *being in spirit and truth,* comes: "I AM, the [one] speaking to you" (4:26). This is, at long last, the seventh husband; the man and the woman are united at this point.[6] His I AM is not different from her I AM. What has been speaking to her all along has been her own I AM—"I am my beloved's and my beloved is mine" (Song 6:3)—the one divine I AM, the Spirit and the Truth. She/he has been "raised up" on the last day, the seventh day, the sabbath day of completion and consummation,[7] in which "all things are shown" (4:25), "everything [the soul] ever did" (4:29), the recapitulation of everything cosmic and psychic in the "ascension to where [he/she] was before" (John 6:62).

Just then the disciples of Jesus return; his efforts and works come back to him, and we realize that the same story that has traced the spiritual development of the woman has been an experience for Jesus as well. What could this experience mean if it is interpreted in terms of *his* journey? She experienced him as coming to her at her moment of readiness. Does he experience her as coming to him at his moment of readiness?

He is tired and comes to the Well. He, too, is thirsty. The day is at its height. He waits. And then she comes, alone, in the bright light. She comes with her sharp-pointed, probing, *leading* questions that force him to the answers. Shall we not regard this shining woman as a Sophia figure, his own Sophia, who has come to meet him at the Well—the very Well at which Jacob met Rebekkah?

Just as the questing soul's story was told in terms of husbands, so Jesus' story can be told in terms of "temptations." "You are those who have continued with me in my temptations" (Luke 22:28)—or trials or tests or tryings, even "tryings-out," experiments, working out the full meaning and implications of the baptismal revelation, "You are my beloved son, in whom I am well pleased." Is he steadily deepening his realization of who he is, what he is to do, what the meaning of it all is? Is he like us in this?

He waits at the Well. He is alone. She comes. She is alone. It is high noon, the fullness of time, the moment of revelation, the hour of solemn weddings. He recognizes that she has come and immediately puts his request to this Wisdom: "Give me to drink."

But she doesn't do it directly. Instead, with her skillfully aimed questions, she provokes and provokes him until she has brought forth from him a full acknowledgment of "how it really is." In this way she not only quenches his thirst but feeds him thoroughly, so that he has no need of further food (John 4:32). He "knows all things and needs none to question him" (John 16:30) more. Was it precisely in order to meet her at the Well that "he had to pass through Samaria" (4:4)?

Now we can reflect on the mystery of this interchange and on the need to "know the gift of God and who it is who is asking for drink" (4:10). The identity of the asker is the crucial point. It is that asker who will receive. Who/ what is it in us that is asking for living water and will not be satisfied with anything less? The mystery figures of the story interchange: She has to know him, know him in herself as her own I AM. He has to know her, know her in himself, as his own Sophia. The asker is the very level of Being in us that will realize itself as I AM, and the gift of God is Sophia, the Holy Spirit, the Spirit of Truth (John 16:13), in whom alone God is to be worshiped (John 4:24) by simply *being*. Only I AM is the Absolute. And it can't be seen or known. It exists only in the subjective case, never the objective. The only way to it is by being it. It has to be the very flow of life within you, the infinite fountain. This is the seventh and true husband, with whom you can be forever united because you always *were* united. It *is* your life, your existence, your selfhood. He says it, speaks it out of its own silence, and she realizes it. They are both fully satisfied. Just at this moment his disciples return. She leaves her water jar and goes back to the city; she will not need to come again to the Well. And he no longer needs that drink, for she has "drawn" the water for him from him; and he doesn't need the material food the disciples have brought, for he is living by a different kind of nourishment.

∞ II ∞

The Ways to Realization

I AM GOING TO TALK about four ways of approach to this mystical realization of God. Not that there are four only, not by any means, but these are four that I have learned something about, mainly from the swamis of the Ramakrishna Order. They are called *yogas*. Yoga means "union," as you can hear in this cognate of other members of the Indo-European family of languages. "Yoke" is kin, too: "Take my yoke upon you"—suppose that meant "take up my yoga," "learn from me." By extension, yoga also means the *way* to the divine union. The four ways that I will point out are the way of work, the way of intellectual insight, the way of control of the mind, and the way of devotion. I put them in that order because I want to conclude with a *bhakti* meditation you can do. If I were to rank them in the order of practice, I would put them as work, devotion, insight, and meditation. I am reminded by this fourfold division of a joke from several decades back. Four members of different religious orders are saying the Divine Office together in a chapel when the lights go out. The Benedictine goes right on saying it, because he knows it by heart; the Franciscan kneels down and prays for light; the Dominican begins a rational inquiry into the cause; and the Jesuit goes out and puts a fuse in!

The Jesuit represents the active approach, so let's start

with that—*karma yoga. Karma* means action, what you do.
Everyone has to engage in action; life itself forces us, says the
Bhagavad-Gita. And for that God sets the example. God sustains the universe. "If I were to cease from work, even for a
moment," says Sri Krishna to Arjuna in the *Gita,* "this whole
world would fall apart. I have nothing to gain from this
work; I expect no reward or gratitude. I do it only out of
love." And we, for our part are allowed to participate in this
divine work, to do our work in imitation of God.

We all have our own proper work. There is endless variety.
We should do our own work, not envying others or despis-
ing them. The incomparable value of the persons doing the
work is in no way dependent on the kind of work they do.
Their value shows in *how* they devote themselves to their
work. Faithfulness to any work with purity of heart will lead
to God in the end.

There is a story about a wandering monk who went into
the forest and practiced certain exercises until he attained
psychic powers. Annoyed by the calling of a crow and a
crane in the tree above his seat, he directed such a baleful
glance their way that they were instantly burned up. Quite
pleased with himself, he went into town to beg for his sup-
per. He entered a courtyard where he called out, "Mother,
give me food." A voice from inside answered, "Wait a little,
my son." The monk thought, "How dare she ask me to wait!
She does not know my power!" At once the voice called out
again, "Don't be thinking too much of yourself, boy. Here
there is neither crane nor crow." He was astonished, and
when she presently brought his food, he asked humbly,
"Mother, how did you know that?"

She answered, "My boy, I do not know your yoga exercises. I am a common, everyday woman. I made you wait
because I was caring for my husband, who is ill. All my life I
have tried only to do my duty in the situation in which I
found myself. That is all the yoga that I practice. But by
doing my duty I have become illumined; thus I could read

your thoughts and know what you had done in the forest. If you want to know something higher than this, go to the market of the next town, where you will find a butcher [lowest caste] who will tell you something you will be very glad to learn."

The monk thought, "A butcher! Why should I do such a thing?!" But his mind had been opened a little and he went. In the market he found a big, fat butcher, cutting meat with big knives and bargaining with people. The monk was appalled: "Is this the man from whom I am to learn?!" But the butcher caught sight of him and said, "Ah, Swami, did that lady send you here? Take a seat until I finish my business." The monk sat, the butcher continued his work, gathered up his money, and then invited the monk to his home. Having seated his guest, he excused himself and went to attend to his aged parents, bathed and fed them and saw to all their wants. Then he came back to the monk and said, "Now, you have come to see me. What can I do for you?" The young monk said that he wanted to understand about God and the self. The butcher gave him a lecture, which forms part of the great poem, the *Mahabharata*, one of the highest flights of Vedanta philosophy. The monk was astonished. "Why are you in that body? With that beautiful knowledge, why are you a butcher, doing such ugly dirty work?"

The butcher replied, "My son, no duty is ugly, none impure. My birth placed me in these circumstances. In this family I learned this trade. I try to do my duty well, and I am unattached. I do not know your yoga, I am not a monk, I have not left the world for the forest. Nevertheless, all that you have heard has come to me through the unattached doing of the duty that has fallen to me."

The message is that whatever our work, it can lead us to the highest realization if we accept it as a religious duty and perform it as worship, without being attached to the fruits of the work. We are always to give our best, unselfishly, doing the work as well as we can, but without any expectation of, or desire for, reward or praise or gratitude. Neither are we to be downcast if, after our best efforts, we are blamed.

What we can learn from this is that such notions as reward and punishment are not helpful or even relevant categories in religion. "Deserving" is to be dropped. We are privileged to do the work itself. The secret of work can be expressed thus: "Let the end and the means be joined into one." Do the work for the sake of working, not for the sake of something else that you hope to get for yourself. Cheerful, wholehearted working for the welfare of others will help us to forget ourselves, go out of ourselves, stop identifying ourselves with our small particular outward descriptions. As these self-thoughts fall away, evaporate, their place is taken by the experienced presence of God. Before very long, we are aware that it is God whom we serve in the other, and then that it is God who is serving, through us.

Jñana yoga is union through knowledge—not academic knowledge, knowledge "about," but experiential knowledge, direct insight. Sometimes *jñana* is defined as discrimination between the real and the unreal. There is a famous prayer: "Lead me from the unreal to the real, lead me from darkness to light, lead me from death to immortality." One prepares for this discrimination by practicing the *karma yoga*, by renouncing all the fruits of one's work in this world and all expectations of reward in the next.

One wants only the Reality Itself, not its manifestations in the pairs of opposites—things good and bad, beautiful and ugly, living and dying, coming into being and passing out of being. Usually we want one of each of these pairs— only the good, the beautiful, existence and life, that which is advantageous to our particular situation and finite being. We pray to a God who is believed to be able to control our experiences and grant us advantageous circumstances and keep away the unpleasant things. But as long as our desires are finite, relative, particular, comparative, we must always accept the other member of the pair as well. After all, that was how we identified the desirable member of the pair— by comparison with the undesirable. By *jñana yoga* we come to a clear realization that in order to be free from the disadvantageous, we must also renounce our insistent desire for the advantageous. It seems that there are no monopoles in the realm of finite being.

The *jñani* therefore practices meditation, holding the mind in calm, dispassionate witness of all reality so that this discrimination can take place without bias or preference. Our mind, in such a practice, separates into two layers—a lower mind and a higher mind. It is like two birds in a fruit tree. The lower bird eats the fruits of the tree, some sweet, some sour or bitter. The higher bird merely sits and looks on. This higher bird represents the Witness-Self, the one who watches the antics of the superficial bird, its pleasures and pains, desires and fears, attractions and aversions.

The Witness-Self learns how this lower mind works and sees that the ultimate truth is not to be found on that plane of consciousness. The Witness-Self then retires into itself and realizes that it does not chase after these experiences that take their character from their contrast with one another and their relations to particular circumstances. The Witness-Self experiences itself as Being and as Consciousness and as Delight in simply being and being conscious. It knows itself as *Sat-Chit-Ānanda.*

This Being that the self is is absolute; it is not being in this way rather than that way. It is unmodified existence, without any particular form. The self's Consciousness is similarly the absolute or ground of knowledge, consciousness without particular concepts to shape and limit it. Its Bliss is the ground state of affectivity, neither pleasure nor pain, the deep tranquillity that remains when all particular forms of affection or disaffection have been removed.

This is what one really is at bottom. It is this Ground which then is modified as particular, finite, relative being, consciousness, and affectivity. The deep self, knowing itself as the ground of the pairs of opposites, knows that this is true of every self, that all selves share in this Ground and on this level are one.

What can we learn from this? When we think they can bear it and are ready, we can encourage people to stop thinking of God as the dispenser of favorable circumstances. We can invite people to open themselves to a love of God that is as unconditional on their parts as they want God's love for them to be unconditional on God's part. We believe that God reveals a love that is not dependent on our beauty or behavior; we say God loves us unconditionally, and we believe that this is a supreme level of being. Similarly, let us try to love God unconditionally, not looking to God to adjust our circumstances or relating to God in terms of our having good luck or bad. Let us be willing to love God equally in our disadvantageous situations as in our pleasant ones.

Let us learn also to turn the mind inward, to enter into our "inner chamber and shut the door" so as to seek the root of our being in secret. When the secret root has been found, it will show, for our life will be transformed. We will no longer identify ourselves in terms of how our conditioned life is shaped. We will live from the ground state rather than the superficial states. We will not believe in ourselves as merely finite, particular beings. We will know that we are rooted in the divine.

An idea that is found in both Hinduism and Buddhism appears at this point. The absolute state, the state of realization, the state of freedom and enlightenment, is *what we now are.* It is not something that we are not and must *become,* something that we *lack* and must *find.* This is why the Buddha said that it was simply a matter of "waking up." We may be reminded of Jesus saying of Jairus's daughter, "She is not dead, she is only asleep." The knowledge of the truth is in us already, we *are* that true knowledge, but it is covered over, as it were. When the heart is purified, we will see God. When we know the truth, we will be free. What we most need to do is to stop telling ourselves that we can't, that we are in darkness, that we are helpless. We are not dead, only asleep. Don't believe people who tell you you are dead and your case is hopeless. Control your mind, turn inward, and see.

There is a Buddhist story about a princess who was quite vain and liked to look at herself in the mirror all the time. Her whole sense of herself was what she saw in the mirror. One day she could not find her mirror, and she ran about crying, "Where is my head? I can't find my head! I've lost my head! Has anyone seen my head?!" Finally, she was made to feel her head from the inside, to realize that the head she sought was the very head that was crying out for the head. She was able to experience *being* the head, as distinguished from *looking at* the head.

What can we learn from this? That which is sought is not different from that which is seeking. The heart that yearns for God is the very heart in which God dwells. St. Augustine's God says to him, "You would not seek me unless you had already found me." I have been here all the time, I have never been away. I have been waiting for you to notice. But by the time we realize *this*, it is no longer clear who is speaking, for the Origin was found at the root of our own inner chamber. God cannot be an object for our sight or intelligence. God is only Subject, I AM. To be united with God means to realize oneself as I AM, to find God's subjectivity in one's own subjectivity, to realize that the spirit that one *is* is the very breath of God in oneself, *as* oneself. If this suggestion rings a bell of truth with us, then we can encourage those with whom we discuss these things to seek God in themselves, not outside, not as somebody else, not as an object vis-à-vis themselves as subject, but as the Soul of their soul, as Reality open and available to them in *subject* terms, God as Subject indwelling themselves as subject. And what we had formerly thought of as ourselves—what we saw in the mirror—will disappear; that which we call "I" now is only the divine Subject in us.

The way to union with God through control of the mind is called *raja yoga,* the royal way. Its textbook is the *Yoga Sutra* of Patanjali, which begins with the definition: "Yoga is the control of thought-waves in the mind." It has eight steps: abstention from evildoing; positive observances; posture; control of breath; withdrawal of the mind from sense objects; concentration; meditation; and absorption in the One Real. When all impurities have been removed by the practice of these disciplines, then our spiritual vision is said to open to the knowledge of God in oneself.

The negative precepts warn us to avoid harming others — this is Gandhi's famous *ahimsa,* nonviolence—avoid false-hood, avoid theft, lust, and greed. All these are developed as rooted in interior dispositions, very much along the lines of the Sermon on the Mount. There are to be no exceptions to our adherence to these rules. The positive precepts are pur-ity, contentment, austerity, study, and devotion to God, again with layers of subtle interpretation.

Patanjali makes some curious comments on these com-mandments. For instance, he says that if we practice stead-fastly the abstention from falsehood, we will become incapable of saying what is not so, and therefore if we say something, it will *be* so! This reminds me of Thomas Aquinas's definition of truth as adequation of thought and thing: when people do it, they make their thoughts conform to the things; when God does it, the things conform to God's thoughts! Also, the Gospel advises that when we pray for anything, we believe that we already have it, and then it will be done!

Abstention from lust gives rise to spiritual power, espe-cially the power to transmit spiritual perception, the essen-tial capacity of a spiritual teacher. For real religion is not "taught" the way school subjects are taught but passed over, as heat or light or any form of energy or power. Caught not taught! Contentment refers to freedom from anxiety and absorption in the present moment; it is the proof that the happiness of God is always within us; whenever we stop inhibiting it, it pours forth. We can promote such contentment by neutralizing painful thoughts, such as anger, desire, fear, egoism, by thought-waves of love, generosity, truth, trust, larger interests. It is interesting that by "study" Patanjali means something very like what our tradition has called *lectio divina:* reading scriptures and the repetition of one's mantram, one of the names of God. Patanjali promises that this practice brings one a vivid sense of the presence of God. This practice is also closely connected with the final admonition, to practice devotion to God. It is that which ultimately leads to union.

When these practices have become well established, one learns posture, which means only to be seated in a position that is firm but relaxed. Its purpose is to enable one to sit still for extended periods and forget one's body. One important detail is that the back be straight so that a clear passage is available from the base of the spine to the top of the head.

The next step is control of *prana*, which I initially called "breath." The word has some of the same ambiguities as the Latin "spirit." It is more usually interpreted as "energy," with a general sense of vitality but also with overtones of subtle powers. It is the dynamic unity of the living body-mind system, exemplified by the physical breath, mediator between the body and its environment, on whose departure the body dies. It can be regarded as a single life-energy, which takes different forms according to which center of operation it is focused in—these are the centers of consciousness that I used as interpretation of the Samaritan woman's "husbands."

There has been a great deal of misunderstanding about postures and breath management in the West. The exercises of *hatha yoga* have been taken to be "yoga" as such; but they have received such emphasis and popularity that they have almost lost their true intent, to prepare a strong body for the rigors of the spiritual path, and have become *distractions* from the spiritual path, confusing aspirants by directing attention to the body and its desirable qualities. It is also important to say that no one should experiment with breathing exercises. One can obtain altered states that way, but that is not spirituality; and there is risk of hallucinations and mental damage.

We will be safer if we think of control of the vital energy in terms of motivation. We have a reservoir of spiritual energy, and if we find the way to liberate it, turn it loose on our spiritual ideal, we will be surprised at the power that is in us. When we touch the aspiration that is rightly *ours*, when we come into contact with that which can draw all our attention, interest, devotion —all our energies—together into one point, then we will be able to work; we will display unexpected wisdom, compassion, and ability to help others. The goal is to keep advancing this ideal of our life to higher and higher centers of consciousness.

As this process is going on, we get to know how our own mind works. We observe our thoughts and feelings as they arise, develop, diminish, disappear. As our motivation-energies concentrate on higher aspirations, we will be less drawn aside or addicted to sense objects or emotional satisfactions. We will be able to observe, to stand apart from, and to control our own interior movements. This is a great advance for most of us in the West, for we usually are simply at the mercy of our feelings, our appetites, fears, emotional needs, and so on. We haven't been brought up to manage these aspects of ourselves. But the mind and the emotions can be trained and tamed just as the movements of the body can be. In the passage where Jesus says "Take my yoke (*yoga*) upon you and learn from me," he adds, "for I am calm, with passions tamed, controlled, and you will find peace for your souls." I have sometimes suggested the image of a double harness, in which we catch the rhythm of a unified life from Jesus, who has the power, because of his *pranic* control, to *transmit* his peace to us. When we are similarly calmed, controlled, and unified, we also will be able to *transmit*.

The final stages of the *raja yoga* are concentration—holding the mind fixed on a single object of regard within one center of consciousness; meditation, an unbroken flow of thought toward this single object; and absorption, wherein the object shines with its own reality and the mind is caught up into it, dissolving the distinction between thinking subject and thought object. The awareness of the Reality of God in this state is far clearer and more real than mere sense experience could ever be, because there is no distortion owing to the influence of various mediators, such as conditions of perception, of the sense organs and nervous system, qualifications owing to ideas and prejudices, and so on. The sudden shift from applying one's own efforts to hold the concentration to finding the Object taking over and overwhelming one has been reported in all spiritual traditions. This is the desired union.

Another account of the stages of the spiritual life is found in the Zen Ox-Herding Pictures. The first picture portrays Starting the Search; the "ox" in question is one's own True Nature. In the second picture we are Finding the Footprints, which corresponds to finding a source of instruction that gives us confidence. Catching a Glimpse of the Ox comes third: a first spiritual experience, in which one has some personal satisfaction that this is a real quest we are on. Catching the Ox indicates that our spiritual experience is strengthened and confirmed; we understand that everything comes from the same source, but we still cannot control ourselves in everyday life; it is an exhausting struggle. The fifth picture shows us Taming the Ox—to a certain extent. In the sixth we are Riding the Ox Home at last, tame and obedient. With the seventh picture the transcendent aspects begin to appear: Ox Lost, Man Remaining—the features of our spiritual training

disappear, our special experiences; we have forgotten all about Zen Buddhism; we are simply in Reality itself from moment to moment. This climaxes with the eighth picture, the empty picture, No Ox, No Man. Ego is gone, circumstances are gone; they arise and disappear together. Picture nine is important: Returning to the Source. The world reappears but is seen from the vantage point of emptiness. The old consciousness has fallen off and we are in the Pure Land. Like the Resurrection, which comes only after the Death. Everything is Buddha; God is all in all. If the stage of Emptiness is the perfection of negative spirituality—taking away all the particulars, whatever is finite, relative—this looking out from a position at the Source is positive spirituality, the Infinite luminously embodied in the transparent finite. Consciousness was in a way suspended in Emptiness; now it is again active, fully aware of itself as Empty, the Nothing that is everything, the circle with center everywhere and circumference nowhere. *Shiva* and *Shakti* are fully wed, the Immutable and the Creative, the Formless and all the Forms. The tenth picture is the fully returned consequence: Entering the City with Helping Hands. The Resurrection follows the Sabbath of the withdrawal of the working, expressive and creative Word—the world in a way comes to an end—and introduces a new working week, rising to fresh life on the First Day.

Reviewing this sequence, we are reminded that we have something very similar in Christianity, the Stations of the Cross. We can read, let us say, the first twelve stations, as stages in our own progress. You might like to experiment with working out the symbolism of the various stations; it makes a good exercise for a retreat experience.[1]

Finally, a brief word about *bhakti yoga*, union with God through devotion, through worship and love. This is the most familiar to us, so we find comparatively few challenges from the East. However, I think there are three worth mentioning. The first is the variety of images and names and relationships under which God may be worshiped. A tradition that has only a single way of representing the Divine and the Absolute will tend to view a tradition with variety as polytheistic. It can be a learning experience to discover that this is not so and to observe that such variety is beneficial to spiritual aspirants. One can regard God as assuming different forms, according to one's sense of oneself and one's relation to God: we may begin as servants of the Supreme Lord or loyal subjects of the Great Sovereign; we may be fearful/hopeful defendants before the Final Judge; we may be trusting patients of the Divine Physician, confident children of a dedicated Parent; we may be eager students of the Teacher, apprentices of the Master, followers of the Leader, the Guide, the Exemplar; we may approach being coworkers; we may be drawn in to be friends; we may be sought and courted as beloved by One whom we likewise seek and yearn for. If these different aspects are represented in our imaginations and in our icons by different figures and names, why should that give any trouble? If some people should be attracted to and should work with one aspect while we are caught up in another, where is the need to quarrel? Variety is good, not bad; to be encouraged, not reduced. Again the lesson is tolerance, acceptance, even nurturance, positive appreciation.

A second challenge that still seems to threaten the West is the popularity in the East of feminine images of God. The Western imagination is so shaped by now in the masculine mode that this seems almost impossible, even ridiculous. Who among us can speak of God as "she" with a straight face? If we pretend to believe that God is Absolute, not really characterized by finite form and human concept, we need to take a good look at this. Being suddenly caught by such an image is useful; it smokes out our failure to live up to our own claims. Unless, of course, we do believe that God is only and definitely male and that any form of femaleness is incapable of representing the Divine Reality. In the East the creative aspect of the Absolute is feminine, the Divine Mother. She is known under several names and assumes various aspects. She is not only productive of the world and protective of it; she is not only compassionate and nurturing, comforting and wise. She is also strong, destructive of evil, awe-inspiring in her transcendent Divinity, overwhelming in her power. She dissolves and consumes the world. She draws the spiritual aspirant to the sublime mysteries and initiates those who are ready. She is immanent in all that exists, present everywhere and always, and she guides the universal process. She is the love in the center of the human heart, the knowledge and wisdom in the human mind, the purity and perseverance in the human will. She is not a second; she *is* the Deity.

A third challenge comes in the Eastern attitude toward the divine incarnation. Buddhism, careful to avoid being distracted or trapped in the tangles of theology, says nothing about this but practices veneration of the various aspects of the Total Reality imaged as "Buddhas," awakened consciousness. But Hinduism has two approaches to offer. Hindu theism—and almost all Hindus are theists, living to God imaged under some particular aspect in a personal way—Hindu theism believes that God has become incarnate many times and will continue to do so, for the correction of the world and the consolation of the devotees. In the *Bhagavad Gita,* Lord Krishna says, "Whenever virtue declines and wickedness prevails, I manifest myself in a human body. To establish righteousness, to destroy evil, to save the good, I come from age to age. . . . Fools deride me who have assumed the human form, without knowing my real nature as the Lord of the universe." This is the *avatara,* the "descent" of God into a worldly form. Such a visitation always initiates a new era. "When a huge flood comes," said Ramakrishna, "all the little brooks and ditches become full to the brim without any effort on their own part; so, too, when an incarnation comes, a tidal wave of spirituality breaks upon the world," everyone is affected. From the Hindu point of view, for one religion to claim that its hero alone is the only incarnation is small-minded in several ways: bigoted, ignorant of world history, unaware of the largeness of God, spiritually undeveloped, immature, and leads to hostility rather than harmony. This is a severe challenge but is one that has to be faced in a world that is truly global now, in which we are all drawing closer together, sharing our lives more and more intimately.

The Hindu approach to divine incarnation takes also another form, sometimes separate from this theistic form and sometimes joined with it in some way. This is the non-dualistic approach. In this view, everyone is divine, everything is divine. When you realize God, when you find the One Real at the center of your own soul, your own consciousness, it is the same One who resides in every apparently separate being. We are all incarnations of God. Everywhere we look, we see nothing but incarnations of God. The universe as a whole is the incarnation of God. You might like to consider which of these two views you find least acceptable and why. Various insights might come from such a consideration.

With these various and complex views available to their devotees, the Easterners enjoy their *bhakti yoga*, yoga of love and devotion and ritualistic worship. Not everyone engages in ritualistic worship; some spiritual aspirants leave it strictly alone and apply themselves only to meditation. Others may not do much with ritual, but they build their lives around their love for God under one aspect or another, and do everything that they do as an act of worship. They cultivate quite vivid senses of the real presence of God with them, participating in all their daily life. An intense interpersonal relationship develops and is consummated in an experience of union, a shared interiority or mutual indwelling of the chosen form of God and the worshiper.

And here another important thing has to be said. All these images, these forms of God, eventually disappear. They were the manifestations of the Formless Absolute and they merge back into it, taking their devotees with them. But meanwhile, the devotees delight in their worship, which they may pursue with art, with song and dance, with poetry. We may take a few minutes now to do our own version of *bhakti* meditation, using various scenes from the Gospel.

We begin with Jesus blessing the children, always an appealing scene. Most of us have seen a picture depicting this occasion: Jesus seated, with children crowding around him and climbing into his lap. "Children were brought to him that he might lay his hands on them and pray. The disciples rebuked the people; but Jesus said, 'Let the children come to me, and do not hinder them; for to such belongs the kingdom of heaven'" (Matthew 19:13-14). If you are still able to connect with your "inner child," you can begin to enter into an affective relation with God from this point of view. We can acknowledge how we long to find ourselves secure in the arms of someone strong and wise and loving, who welcomes us and protects us and caresses us. We can begin our love for God with a child's love. Jesus validates it, encourages it. He himself relates to God as to an intimate parent, calling his divine Father "Abba," the name the child uses at home—equivalent, the scholars tell us, to our "Papa."

This child's love finds such security and develops so much reverence and devotion for the divine parent that it rapidly grows into an adult's dedication and loyalty to a venerated Father. This is what we see in Jesus, in his obedience and his availability to the indwelling Father. He makes himself transparent so that the Father may shine through him. He does only what the Father urges him to do, speaks what the Father gives him to speak. This is his devotion in action.

Jesus offers the same warm, blessing love to his grown-up friends as he gave the trusting children. In the kingdom of heaven, we are all to be like that, open, unself-conscious, expecting and giving concrete affection. His words are full of consolation and strength. He opens wider worlds, affirms and elevates us, reverses our negative and energy-robbing self-images and beliefs. The Sermon on the Mount is replete with this. What confidence he has in us! What great expectations! He believes we are capable of tremendous things, and because he believes so in us, we begin to believe, too. "You are the light of the world! Don't hide your light, let it shine! When people see your good works, they will give glory to your Father in heaven." "You are capable of great things. You are called to a more profound purity and spirituality than the simple keeping of the Law, necessary though that is. God has blessed you and called you to enter his kingdom of heaven. Its righteousness exceeds that of this generation of teachers, but you are ready for it , you can do it. You can revise many of your ideas and feelings, you can expand your life and your love until you become like your heavenly Father, who does not recognize any difference between friends and enemies, but treats all alike. You are going to be able to live the divine life in its completeness." "Your piety will be interior, simple, and sincere, coming from the heart, with no ulterior motive. You will be in no doubt about where the treasure of your life is to be found. Your vision will be single, focused, clear, bright! You will so well see how you are related to God that you will have no anxieties. You will not be moved to criticize, judge, or fear. You will know that all you seek will be given you, for your Father is bountiful and loves you dearly."

Hearing such words, our hearts begin to burn with love for this teacher, for the God he reveals, for the meaningfulness of our life, the vision he exposes to us, the hope and confidence he arouses in us. He enables us to see ourselves, God, the world in such a different way. He is infectious, vitalizing. When we are with him, we feel alive, capable of the great things he sees in us, able to love all, to live a divine life. He is funneling divine life to us. We mustn't lose him; we must stay with him.

And so we run after him. "Jesus turned and saw them following, and said to them, 'What do you seek?' And they said to him, 'Rabbi, where are you staying?' He said to them, 'Come and see.' They came and saw where he was staying; and they stayed with him that day" (John 1:38–39). This is the crucial point in the yoga of love: the resolve to *stay* with the Beloved and the discovery of where the Beloved "stays." Accepting Jesus' invitation, we come and we see. We see and we stay. We move into Jesus' home and start living with him. Think what that means! We can imagine, in meditation, what that might be like, the closeness, the detail of daily life shared, the deepening of the relationship, coming to know one another thoroughly. And we can know it, without imagining it in meditation, by seeing that it is equivalent to having Jesus move into *our* home and *our* life, and we become alive in this consciousness in our own concrete daily experiences. We strive now to have *bhakti* consciousness always, suffusing everything we do. We try to remember the presence of Jesus always with us, his warm, strengthening love for us, our glowing, eager, yearning love for him.

And in this *bhakti yoga,* this union through love, we begin to be aware of "where he stays." And we know that we are intended to "stay" there, too. We know he prays, "Father, I desire that they also, whom you have given me, may be with me where I am, to behold my glory which you have given me in your love for me, before the foundation of the world" (John 17:24). The "where I am" is somewhere not measured by the dimensions of this world. It belongs to the reality that is "before the foundation of the world." There is "glory" there, glory that comes from God's love and is eternal. And we are to be "there" too. This is to come about by our "staying" with him. We will stay "where" he stays, in that realm of love-glory. Now.

Don't think you can't do it. You can live in both worlds: rooted in the glory-world, you can walk about in the daily-work world, and some of that glory will shine through you, from you. You can do it, you can walk on water, as long as you keep your eye on Jesus and believe in his confidence in you, his vision of sharing this divine glory of God's love with you. That's what he's doing, living in both worlds, and he assures us we can do it too, just as he does. We learn how to do this, we *grow into* doing this by staying with him, staying with his love, with his vision, with his prayer.

When we do this, we become like Mary of Bethany, who sits with Jesus and his other friends, listening to him and talking of the kingdom of God. "A woman named Martha received him into her house. And she had a sister called Mary, who sat at the Lord's feet and listened to his teaching. . . . The Lord answered her, 'Martha, you are anxious and troubled about many things; few things are needed, or even only one. Mary has chosen the good part, which shall not be taken from her'" (Luke 10:38–42). When we resolve to "stay" with Jesus, he protects us and will not let us be taken from him. The *bhakti* consciousness has reached that continuous adherence that Patanjali described as "an unbroken flow of thought." The "good part" is now in the center of our life-reality; we are rooted in it, we "stay" there. Whereas we once had to make an effort to maintain our *bhakti*, now the Lord maintains it. There is no risk of losing it. We are soaking up his atmosphere, drawing his being into ourselves—"eating" and "breathing" him —and he is likewise absorbing us. We are so growing into a single Life that it will not be *possible* to separate us. This is his will, that we should be "with" him, where he is, seeing, participating in, his glory. His glory, we find, is expressed in his total self-givingness, his pouring out all that he is, "laying down" his life for his friends.

An unidentified woman now appears in another scene, showing our entering into this self-emptying glory. "As he sat at table, a woman came with an alabaster phial of ointment of pure nard, very costly, and she broke the phial and poured it over his head. But there were some who said, 'Why was the ointment thus wasted? For this might have been . . . given to the poor.' And they reproached her. But Jesus said,

'Let her alone; why do you trouble her? She has done a beautiful thing to me. . . . She has anointed my body beforehand
for burial. And truly I tell you, wherever the gospel is
preached in the whole world, what she has done will be told
as a memorial to her'" (Mark 14:3–9).

We are represented in this scene as nameless; we are no
longer distinguishing ourselves from the Divine or from its
self-emptying and pouring out. This is shown in the break-
ing of the phial and the pouring out of the costly perfume.
This is what happens in the soul of the *bhakta*, the one who
loves: it breaks open and all its love pours out. It is this way
with Jesus, it is this way with his devotee who has entered
into him and is "staying" with him "where he is," sharing his
life.

Frequently there is complaint about *bhaktas*, about those
who are absorbed in the contemplative life instead of being
engaged in social service to the poor. Service to the poor
should always be done, but there is a place also for this great
love directly for God. It is "a beautiful thing" and again is
protected by Jesus, who accepts it as participation in his own
outpouring life, his "glory." He goes so far as to proclaim a
memorial for this archetypal *bhakta*, that this great love shall
always be preached and never be forgotten. John's version of
this story adds that "the fragrance of the ointment filled the
whole house" (John 12:3)—"wherever the gospel is preached
throughout the whole world." This is the significance of the
bhakta's devotion. Far from being a "waste," its beauty fills
the whole world, carrying divine love into every part.

There are two more images to show how thoroughly the
bhakta is joined in yoga, in union, with the Lord of Love. The
first occurs when Jesus proposes to "go again into Judea,"
where he had narrowly escaped being stoned. His disciples
urge the danger of this path, but "Thomas the Twin says to
his fellow disciples, 'Let us also go, that we may die with
him'" (John 11:16). Now we are seeing the fulfillment of the
oft-repeated statement in the New Testament: "Whoever

seeks to save his life will lose it; and whoever loses his life for my sake and the gospel's will save it" (Mark 8 :35). The great paradox of love appears subjectively: the more we give ourselves away, the more we are ourselves, the wider is our life. But the giving has to be thorough. You cannot love "father or mother"—whatever has made you what you are—more than the Lord of Love, nor can you love "son or daughter"— whatever you have produced—more (Matthew 10:37). Nevertheless, pouring out, "laying down," your life in its entirety is essential to the Good News, to being immortal and divine. You are united with what God as Love is doing.

And this is the vision that Thomas the Twin has in the end, when he sees Jesus as wounded humanity and as glorified divinity, and sees these two as one: "My Lord and my God!" (John 20:28). This is the paradox of Love as objective: Infinitude and finitude, the Eternal and the temporal, Creator and creature, united. This is the culmination of the Yoga of Love.

The Search for the Self

PROBABLY THE CLEAREST and strongest teaching to come out of the East is the insistence that the place to look for Reality is in the Self. Original Cartesians in their own right, Easterners point out that the one bit of Reality that we have sure hold of is our own consciousness. You can't ask questions about Reality without being real yourself. So, if you want to get to the foundations of Reality, the best way to go—indeed the only *sure* way to go—is through your own self.

Of course, not everyone is interested in getting to the foundations of Reality. Some people want only to make themselves more comfortable, to find a way of easing the strains of embodied existence. They have no overpowering urge to find out *how it is*. There are also those who want to make the world better, which is a kind of in-between position. But, if either the ease-seekers or the world-betterers pursue their purposes relentlessly, seeking the most general solution for every person and situation, they will be forced to try to get close to the foundations of Reality. And when they do that, they will have to go into the self. For it is only the self that suffers and asks for relief; it is only the self that perceives the world as "world" and understands what "better" means. When we meet people in the retreat situation, we meet all these types. A useful thing we can learn from the East is to discern what the purposes of our retreatants are. But the retreat *director*, the *guide*, has to be acquainted with the paths to the foundations of Reality through the self. So say the teachers from the East.

Religion, as we understand it, is not yet dealing with the fundamental issues, they would say. According to the *Mundaka Upanishad*, "Considering religion to be observance of rituals and performance of acts of charity, the deluded remain ignorant of the highest good" (1.2:10). So the yogas we spoke of in the previous chapter, especially *karma yoga* and *bhakti yoga*, works and worship, are here adjudged insufficient. They are acceptable as preparatory, but beyond a certain stage they become impediments. Even theology and the concern for orthodoxy do not carry us to the end. The foundation of our existence and our thinking is not an object to be mastered by the categories of our understanding. So the Eastern teacher looks perhaps indulgently on quarrels over points of doctrine that seem so important to theologians and says to them, "The God you are arguing about exists only in your own minds, it is only a concept and a set of propositions you yourselves have created and passed down from generation to generation! How can you devote yourselves so seriously to such things?! The Reality you should be seeking has to be quite beyond all this."

We are going to continue talking in terms of concepts, even when we urge that the concepts are woefully inadequate. What else can we do? But at least we can understand and perhaps accept that, like the bride in the Canticle (Song of Solomon), it is only when we have gone a little beyond the guardians of the city that we find the one whom our soul loves.

So, what can we say about the search for the Self, for the Foundation of Reality through the self? First, I believe it may be helpful to point out that the word "I" does not have a single clear, obvious, and fixed referent. This is probably not a familiar notion to many Westerners. For the most part, we seem to assume that there is no need to ask What do you mean? when someone says "I." It means the one who experiences, the one who acts, and especially the one who is responsible, who can be praised or blamed, rewarded or punished. Even when there is talk of the "false self" and the "true self," it is my impression that most people in that conversation think that the "false self" is a social façade or possibly a self-image that has been projected onto us by our social environment. The "true self" is our genuine personality, the feelings, attitudes, and capabilities that sincerely characterize us as historical human beings. In other words, the self is the body, mind, and social relations of the human being. That is not what the Eastern spiritual masters mean by the Self.

So one of the things we can learn from them, or a way in which we can be challenged by them, lies in the area of what is meant by the Self. If we can become aware that the word "I" does not have an obvious and fixed referent, this will help a great deal. Instead of quarreling over whether this or that is the true Self, we can see that "self" may mean different things in different contexts, and especially it will mean different things at different stages of our spiritual development. And that is the essential point. For it may be that spiritual development can be succinctly described as the transmigration of the sense of self.

In the Christian tradition, we have some clues to this path in the various reported utterances of Jesus, speaking of himself in relation to what he calls his "Father." I have arranged these texts in order of progressive initiative and advancing sense of union with the Father. At one point he says, "Why do you call me good? No one is good but God." Then he says "I do nothing of myself, but the Father dwelling in me performs his works." This is followed by "I do as the Father commands me" and that by "I do what I see the Father doing" and then "I do always the things that please Him." Finally he says, "Whoever sees me sees the Father; the Father and I are one." The referents of the word "I" in these speeches are not the same. This is the point that is of interest in our search for the Self. In the Eastern view, the only one of them that is really the Self is the last one, the one the identifies the Self with the Source.

It is a matter of shifting the location of the sense of identity. What needs to be avoided, from this point of view, is first assuming that "I" refers to just one fixed referent and then debating which of the above statements is the correct one: Should we say "I do nothing of myself," or say "Who sees me sees the Father"? This debate can drop out of the picture as soon as we give up the assumption that the sense of identity is fixed, that "I" always means the same. All of them will be true at the successive stages of spiritual development.

There are various ways of ranging the senses of self that we experience. One way can be regarded either as chronological development or as concentric shells of our being at any time. It works like this: the outermost shell, or the first level of identity, is the body. When the young child says "I," the body is indicated. This description of the self continues into adulthood with our concern for the appearance of the body and its ability to perform. The next shell in is the emotional sense of our experience and our relationships. When we say "I" on this level, we are locating ourselves in our emotional experiences. Beyond that is the stage of identifying with the mind—our memories, our perceptions, our opinions. Perhaps many of us stop there. Asked who we are, we usually describe ourselves in terms of our nationality, work, religion, marital status, parenthood, political affiliation, then maybe our interests, talents, avocations, even perhaps our handicaps and outstanding social differences. The trouble in our life, the Eastern teacher says, is precisely that we do identify with these levels of experience. All of them are subject to change, they are dependent on events outside themselves, they are relational, characterized by contrast, therefore finite. The Real Self has to be something that is independent, absolute, infinite, something that is in itself. It is only by finding That One that we can be assured of immortality.

Above the level of the mind, or more inward, or discovered later in our development, is the Intellect: the power of distinguishing truth from falsehood, reality from illusion, and seeing directly into the nature of being. This enables us to see that everything else in experience has to be founded on the conscious Self. And that ultimate Self cannot itself be dependent, relative, and finite, for it has to be the ground of, the perceiver of, all the finite beings. The Ground Consciousness has no particular character, no description, no form, for it is what receives all forms. Consciousness itself is not the *content* of consciousness. The Intellect sees that this must be so. When we identify with this level of our being, then we know that the real Self must be this contentless Consciousness and/or the Source from which it has sprung, and that we must search for it.

When we succeed from time to time in sinking into that unmodified consciousness, especially when we are no longer identifying ourselves as the one experiencing a particular pleasure or pain, then we are aware of ourselves as "bliss." The more we eliminate descriptions, the more we liberate ourselves; when we stop limiting ourselves to being this way rather than that, then we become vast. The more we empty ourselves of predicates, the more we become full beings. When we cease to put some restriction after our name, I AM, and leave it simply as I AM, without modification, then we realize our status as child of God, called by God's own Name.

"The ultimate aim of the yoga processes," says Surendranath Dasgupta of Presidency College, Calcutta, in *Hindu Mysticism* (1927), "is to dissociate ourselves from our sensations, thoughts, ideas, feelings, etc., to learn that these are extraneous associations, foreign to the nature of the Self but adhering to it almost so inseparably that the true Self cannot be easily discovered as a separate and independent entity." The Self is the ultimate principle of pure consciousness, distinct from all mental functions, faculties, powers, or products. But, Dasgupta points out, we have confused it with our mental and emotional contents. The mental operations, he says, "usurp the place of the principle of pure consciousness so that it is only the mind and the mental operations of thought, feeling, willing, which seem to be existing, while the ultimate principle of consciousness is lost sight of." If we designate the true Self as "spirit" and call all the particular functions collectively "mind," then we may say that "it is the mind and its activities by which the true nature of the spirit seems to be obscured."[1]

Now I will give you an example of how I think I learn something from this for purposes of reformulating it in terms of our tradition. We pick up the idea that the thoughts, feelings, ideas, opinions, habits, customs, and so on of the mind can obscure the reality of the spirit, usurp its place, fail to acknowledge it. A familiar text in the Gospel says of the Incarnate Word that he came to his own and his own did not receive him. And the stories of Jesus are full of accounts and remarks indicating opposition, hostility, failure to accept. There is a tendency in places to set up a frankly polemical attitude between Jesus and his "enemies." This is felt by many of us as an embarrassment, especially because this attitude, when directed toward actual *people* and carried into social and political practice, has been responsible for serious injustices and some of the most grievous tragedies we have known. It would be an advantage, therefore, if we could interpret these texts in terms of the aspects of everyone's inner life that prevent us from opening fully to the spirit, the Self.

A good example would be the resurrection story which begins by saying that the disciples of Jesus were gathered together in the upper room and its doors were shut for fear that their enemies might attack them. Jesus is the spirit, the Self; his disciples are consciousness currents drawn to him, gathered together in concentration in the upper room, the highest consciousness so far attained. The doors of this consciousness are tightly shut so that no distraction or temptation to identify with the merely mental operations can penetrate. In this situation the glorious Christ appears *within* the chamber, not *coming in.* It shows itself when the doors are securely shut and when the consciousness within is "gathered." It brings "peace" and declares that it is "I," the real Self. The forerunner of this revelation is the advice of Jesus, in his instruction on prayer, to "go into your inner chamber and *shut the door,* and pray to your Father in secret." The inner chamber, of course, is the innermost part of our consciousness. Shutting the door again means refusing distractions or finite identifications, silencing the mind. Father means Source of Being, and praying in secret means without words or concepts.

The search for the Father is the search for the Source is the search for the Self, if we take up the Eastern view. Again I remind you that this is by no means your everyday self. If you believe that you are your everyday self, then you don't know the Father yet. You need to go deeply and secretly into your inner chamber and seek your Source. In the eighth chapter of the Gospel of John, Jesus says, "If I glorify myself, my glory is nothing." It is not the superficial self, the everyday self, the embodiment, that is of itself glorious. "It is my Father who glorifies me." The Source of all Being, which dwells within, the deep Self, the pure I AM without modification—that is the source of all glory. "Of whom you say that he is your God, but you have not known him." You know there is God, you know that your finite existence is dependent on that God. But you don't yet know that One as your own Source, that out of which your being is even now springing, that which is, as St. Augustine said, more intimate to you than you are, yourself—that is, if you identify with the superficial, descriptive self. But the spirit of God deep within you cries out—if only we could hear and believe—"I know him! If I said, I do not know him, I should be a liar . . . but I *do* know him."

I think that something like this is the challenge from the East. Deep in ourselves is the true Self, and that true Self is not separate from, or even different from, the Source of Being, what you call your God. That true Self in us says, "I do know him." "Why can you not understand what it is saying?" Jesus asks. "It is because you cannot bear to hear this word." The suggestion from the East is that we go into our inner chamber and shut the door and listen for this word, this cry from the deep Self, this affirmation and claim, that we see if we can bear to hear it. See if we can hear the Self declare, "I do know him, the Source. The Father and I are one."

This is what the *Upanishads* call the union of *Atman* and *Brahman*. The Ground of Being and the Ground of Consciousness, the I AM of all Reality and the I AM deep in you, what you call your God and what I call my Father, are not two, cannot be torn apart. When you know this—really know it by direct inner experience—then you will know who you are and that you are immortal, that you can never die. This is the truth that makes you free. This is liberation. This is what the guru imparts to a disciple who is undergoing the initiation into *samnyasa*, which means laying everything totally aside. Compare the Christian notion of leaving all things and following Christ.

There is a beautiful description of the *samnyasa* ceremony by Swami Abhishiktananda in his book *The Further Shore*.[2] Swami Abhishiktananda was a French Benedictine monk, Father Henri LeSaux (died 1973), who emigrated to India and adopted the lifestyle of a Hindu monk. He was deeply attracted to the silent meditative life, to total renunciation, and to the experience of the nondual Reality. If asked what we can learn from the East, he would probably say *samnyasa* and *Advaita*, renunciation and nondualism. *Samnyasa*, he says, "remains the most radical witness to that call to the beyond which sounds, however faintly, in the heart of every [person]." It is "the sign" of that which "is beyond all signs," which "lies beyond all possibility of being adequately expressed by rites, creeds, or institutions." One of the great things we can learn from the East is that a religion that really has insight into the Ultimate will point to the necessity for transcending itself, going beyond its doctrines and practices. *Samnyasa* is that which does not bear the name of any religion or spiritual path. "It corresponds to a powerful instinct, so deep-rooted in the human heart, . . . that it is anterior to every religious formulation."

In the *samnyasa* initiation the candidate makes the following affirmations:

> I have renounced all worlds: earth, heaven, and all worlds in between, whether mental, emotional, or the esoterically "spiritual." My total dedication is to the Infinite Self.
>
> I have left behind all desires, for progeny, for riches, for any finite place of identity.
>
> Let no creature have fear of me, for I am united with That from which everything comes.

The guru exhorts him: "Arise, wake up, you who have received the blessing. Keep awake!" (We may be reminded of the liturgical verse from the Epistle to the Ephesians: "Awake, O sleeper, and rise from the dead; and Christ will give you light " [5:14], as well as of Mark's admonition, "What I say to you, I say to all: Stay awake!" [13:37].) This is followed by intoning the hymn:

> I know him, that supreme Person, beyond all darkness; only in knowing him does one overcome death; there is no other way. In total serenity he rises up from this body, reaches the highest light, and is revealed in his own proper form; he is the supreme Person; he is Atman, the Self; he is Brahman, Ground of All. He is the All, he is the Truth, he is beyond fear, beyond death. He is unborn. And I myself am He.

The candidate then casts away all clothing, every mark of identification or belonging to any caste or religion, and is wrapped anew in a flame-colored cloth (reminiscent to us, perhaps, of the Spirit of Pentecost). After a few final instructions—remember your freedom, remain united with the Spirit, centered in the Self, absorbed in the inner mystery of the nondual Brahman—the guru imparts, with all the spiritual power the guru has, the four Great Words:

> OM! Brahman is consciousness. (*Aitreya Upanishad* 5.3)
> OM! Atman is Brahman. (*Mandukya Upanishad* 2)

The disciple repeats these two utterances after the guru. But the third is spoken by the guru alone:

> OM! Thou art That! (*Chandogya Upanishad* 6.8.7)

And the new samnyasin alone replies:

> OM! I am Brahman. (*Brihadaranyaka Upanishad* 1.4.10)

With a last blessing the guru sends the *samnyasin* away, "across the infinite space of the heart, to the Source. Go to the Unborn, yourself unborn . . . which you yourself have found and from which there is no returning." Immediately the initiate, recognizing that "the time of departure is at hand," sets out on what the *Brihadaranyaka Upanishad* calls "the ancient narrow path" (4.4.8), which, Jesus confirms, leads to life but is found by but few (Matthew 7:14).

Swami Abhishiktananda was deeply influenced by Sri Ramana Maharshi, whom he met in South India in 1950, the year before Ramana died. Sri Ramana was a most unusual case: he realized the Self at the age of seventeen without any instruction from anyone, simply by imagining that his body was dead and asking himself intensely what was left. At that time, he says, "I had never heard of Brahman. . . . I did not yet know that there was an Essence or impersonal Real underlying everything and that Ishvara (the God who makes and governs the universe) and I were both identical with it. Later . . . as I listened to the *Ribhu Gita* and other sacred books, I learnt all this and found that the books were analysing and naming what I had felt intuitively without analysis or name."[3]

Assured by his own direct experience that he himself was not the body and had nothing to fear from the condition or death of the body, Ramana left home and went to live in the Temple of Siva near Mt. Arunachala, where gradually devotees collected around him and an ashram was built to accommodate them all; this ashram is still operating and Sri Ramana's teachings are available in books.

Sri Ramana's teaching could hardly be simpler. You *are* the Self, nothing but the Self. Know that, abide in that, and be free. It is not something to be attained; it is what cannot be avoided. Everything else depends on the Self. It is covered over with thoughts, and the thoughts project/represent the world. But all this takes place on the ground of the Self. Therefore, ask repeatedly, "Who am I?" and pass beyond the contents of the mind to that which is the eternal Witness of all, the unconditioned "I." This is the direct method to silence the mind; it is the first and last question—all other analysis and speculation is unnecessary. Use the mind to see where the mind rises from; it is only after the rise of the thought of "I" that other thoughts can arise. Therefore, seek the source of that "I" thought. But do not *think about* it. Concentrate on the sense of being, the feeling of "I AM," and thus exclude all thoughts "about" anything, even the Self. Fix this concentrated attention in the heart of your being and abide there. Even in your work remain rooted there. You are the *Seer;* do not identify with the *seen.* What is finally realized as a result of such inquiry into the Source of our sense of "I am" is the undifferentiated Light of Pure Consciousness, into which the reflected light of the mind is completely absorbed.

This Reality of Pure Consciousness is eternal by its nature.

This is what a friend of Abhishiktananda told him vigorously, and it was always to him the strongest challenge:
"Who realizes . . . the Self? That is all a matter of words. The
Atman cannot be 'reached.' Who reaches the Self, except the
Self? 'Nonrealization' is simply an excuse that one gives for
trying to escape from the Real and continuing to lead with a
clear conscience a stunted life of prayers, devotions and even
asceticism, all no doubt very satisfying to the little ego but in
fact utterly useless. Has the sun really set, merely because I
have closed the shutters? The fundamental obstacle to realization is precisely the notion that this realization is still
awaited."[4] We might want to ask at this point whether this is
what Jesus was saying to Martha about the resurrection: It is
not at "the end of the world," something to be indefinitely
awaited; it is now—"I AM the Resurrection and the Life."

Abhishiktananda's friend went on, "The Truth has no
'Church.' The Truth is the Truth, and it cannot be passed on
to others by anyone at all. The Truth shines with its own
light. . . . For anyone who has seen the Real, there is neither
Christian, Hindu, Buddhist, or Muslim. There is only the
Atman, and nothing can either bind or limit or qualify the
Atman. There is only one thing you need, and that is to break
the last bonds that are holding you back. You are quite ready
for it. Leave off your prayers, your worship, your contempla-
tion of this or that. Realize that *you are*."[5]

I thought you might like to have a little experience of the
sort of thing that is being proposed here as spiritual practice.
In a way this is ridiculous, since we will do it for only five
minutes. And in a way it is quite right, for time has nothing
to do with it and there is nothing to be attained, for you
already are, always have been, and always will be the Self. It
is a matter of clearing away the obstacles that are attracting
our attention away from this truth. So try to turn your mind
inward. You will see at first all the thoughts. See that you
yourself are not the thoughts. You may think, "I am my

body." See that you are the thinker of that thought, and that the body, compacted of dust and destined to return to dust, is not You. Similarly with your personality. The images of your personality reflected to you from your social relations are modifications of your fluctuating mind. Even the mind is not You, much less this personality. You are the One thinking those thoughts. You are the One who doubts, You are the One who resists. You are the One who knows that you are the one who doubts and resists. Be that Knower, but know nothing but that you are the Knower. Everything else in your experience appears in yourself as the Experiencer. Be the Experiencer. Behind the Experiencer is the One Who Is. Be the One Who Is, whether there is experience going on or not. Stay there, being your act of existing, prior to all thoughts, to all notions of what you are in a finite way. Be the I AM. Now sink down into that pure I AM, without any object before the mind, and feel for its Source. It comes up into your I AM *as* your I AM; it is not an object that appears before the mind. It is that on which all else depends, that which remains when all else disappears, that which alone is Real in its own right. Let yourself be steady in this Reality. It is the Origin of all being. It is the Being-ness of your being. Therefore, you *are* That.

The Mystery of Nondualism

I have escaped and the small self is dead;
  I am immortal, alone, ineffable;
I have gone out from the universe I made,
  And have grown nameless and immeasurable
I am the one Being's sole immobile Bliss;
  No one I am, I who am all that is.[1]

THE POEM is by Sri Aurobindo Ghose, twentieth-century yogin and philosopher of Pondicherry in India. It expresses the sense of nonseparation, nondifference, nondualism, that characterizes what some people consider to be the highest reaches of Eastern spirituality. This is the hardest challenge to accept, even to admit that the claim of nondualism has to be taken seriously. This is why it should not be mentioned until it is overwhelmingly clear that the finite ego-self is not the ground of the experience and the claim to nondual union with the Ultimate.

It is again a matter of experience. There are people who insist that they know from experience that in the highest state all distinction between themselves and the Ultimate Reality, or God, disappears entirely—in fact, that it is obvious that such distinction makes no sense, has no possible reality, and that the appearance of such distinction and separation is delusion or ignorance.

We might reflect that we have no need to go to the East to learn this, and cite the exchange between Jesus and Philip in the Fourth Gospel: Philip demands, as a final appeal, "*Show us the Father* [the Source, the Origin, the total Account of the Whole Thing], and we will be satisfied." Jesus replies, in effect, "Open your eyes! You're always looking at the Father. How can you say, Show us the Father? Whoever sees me, sees the Father." You have only to omit the restriction of this claim to Jesus alone and take him as paradigm of all reality, to have something very similar to what our friends from the Orient are confessing.

Perhaps we would dare to suggest that this is what Jesus is revealing to Nicodemus by telling him that anyone who aspires to ascend to heaven must have been born from above and come down from heaven in the first place, must be a spiritual reality, born of the Spirit. This is, in fact, the position of the children of humanity, who *are* always rooted in heaven, if they only knew it. "That which is born of the Spirit *is* Spirit." You should *know* this if you're a teacher in a religious tradition.

If we take the nondual suggestion seriously and search through the Gospels, we can find quite a lot of places in which this perspective appears, especially if we interpret Jesus as paradigm for the rest of us, "like us in *all* things, sin alone excepted," or turned around, *we* are like *him* in all things. The insistence on I AM in the Fourth Gospel is the strongest presence of this perspective if you choose to take it that way. The tense is present, *always* present. Just as "what is born of the flesh is flesh," so what happens in time is temporal; it's not a question of a "second" birth, "again," but of an *eternal* birth "from above." You can't *start* to be eternal.

But you can realize it suddenly. And that's the nature of the spiritual experience we're talking about. Master Rinzai, of the Zen Buddhist tradition, says "It is not that I under-stood from the moment I was born of my mother, but that after exhaustive investigation and grinding discipline, in an instant I realized my True Nature."[2] Being born of one's mother is flesh from flesh. Realization brings to light the eternal Truth of the Spirit. If you break out of identifying with the flesh—if you "die"—you simultaneously realize birthlessness and deathlessness and know that you will never die. Is this what "believing in Jesus" means? Does it mean seeing him as the Paradigm, the Example not only of *what to do* but of *how it is*, the Revelation to us of our True Nature? When you "believe in him" do you know that you will never die, because you know that you, like him, are a child of God, born of the Spirit, therefore a spiritual being, eternal in the heavens?[3]

Jesus complains frequently that the people to whom he is trying to make his revelation can't "hear" him because they continue to identify with the flesh, with worldly relations and ambitions, with time and finitude. It is only the Spirit in us that can hear the spiritual message. We can't hear it until we to some extent know that *we are* the Spirit. The Spirit doesn't have form; it is like the wind, without origin, without destination, blowing free, invisible. Yet it is our self, luminous. The contemporary American roshi, Eido Tai Shimano, asks, What *can* expound the Dharma—the Revelation, the Spiritual Truth that frees—what *can* listen to it? "This very *you*, standing before me *without any form*, just shining."[4] This is nondualism, Buddhist style.

Let's talk about that for a while, with the help of Eido Roshi. The eighteenth-century Japanese Zen Master Hakuin says that we are "fundamentally Buddha." We are awake, but we don't think we are, we don't feel that we are; we experience fear and guilt and discontentedness. That is why we practice, that is why we sit—to clarify our sense of who we really are. When we become hungry enough for the truth, "when we have Great Curiosity for the Really Real," then "we bite. And this biting is zazen," sitting meditation.

What happens then is not unlike what we heard from Sri Ramana. Eido says that "we do zazen, asking deeply, What is my True Nature? Where is it?" In the beginning, we think, "I'm practicing, I'm doing zazen." But gradually we begin to realize that there is Something, Something that was there before we were born (according to the flesh) and will still be there after the temporal being we identify with is here no more, Something that is "constantly active." At first we think of It as being different from ourselves, being somewhere else, but as we discover It as boundless, beginningless, endless, unaccountable, we find that It cannot be absent from us or contrasted with us. It is Here. It cannot be different from us, and therefore we cannot be different from It. We experience It living and active in the very center of our own being.[5] And we experience It, as Ramana also said, as "formless." As Jesus also said? All of you, children of the Spirit, are like the wind, formless. The Spirit, called in Buddhism "Mind" with a capital M, is "without form." But this has to be experience, not words, not theory, not doctrine.

From the Buddhists we can learn that this "formlessness" of Mind, of the Spirit, can be experienced in a certain context which they call *anatta*. It means not–substance, not an entity. I think this is a crucial point to grasp. I was helped by the saying, "Only causative linkages, no individual entities." And it helped that I had been studying systems, self-organizing, adaptive, emergent systems. The point about the systems is that by the *interaction* of their functional components a phenomenon arises of the whole simultaneous net of interactions, a phenomenon that has so much identifiable character as a whole that we can validly deal with it *as if* it were an entity in itself. Let me give you some examples: a candle flame seems to have a definite shape—you can recall it, you could draw a picture of it right now. But you know that there isn't any set *being* there, only the moving stream of glowing bits of carbon flying off the burning wick. They glow because of the interaction "burning"; they rise because of the interaction "gravity"; they become invisible at the tip of the "flame" because of the interaction "heat dispersion." But such apparent entities can be manipulated as if they were beings in themselves. Take, for example, the electron beam that scans your television set. The "beam" is again a moving stream of particles, but the "beam" as such can be pulled this way or that and bent by applying a magnetic field to it. The television picture itself is another instance. Figures appear and hold together as wholes, and we perceive them as identifiable entities, but they are really just moving electrons, constantly and rapidly scanning the surface of the screen. The *relations* among the scintillating particles of the screen create the image, the *phenomenon*, the "appearing" of the picture, which nevertheless can be dealt with—perceived, adjusted, reasoned about, and so on— as if it were a being in its own right. Living bodies are the next example. They are all "dissipative systems": they take in matter, energy, and information from their environments, organize these into their own characteristic forms, and dissipate the useless, the surplus, or the applied matter, energy, information. They seem to be definite *beings*, but they are *traffic flows*, highly complex nets of *interactions. Our* bodies are such traffic loops. And so are our personalities, composed of nets of interactions on the social plane with other systems like ourselves. When we begin to see what is going on from this point of view, our sense of identity has to undergo a significant transformation. We had thought "we" meant our bodies and our personalities, our minds (small m), our characters. Now we see that all these are flowing systems of interactions with other centers of flow of similar levels of organization, or simpler.

All the traffic flows are governed by causal regularities, what the West calls natural law and what the East calls

karman, action. The appearance of bounded beings is due to
the consistency of the patterning of the flows. Their stability
is not forever but it is, in many cases, long-lasting enough for
us to deal with these "emergent phenomena" as if they were
fixed beings. But there are not really any such beings-in-
themselves there, only the interactions. I think this is what is
being said in the *Wisdom Sutra:*

> All phenomena are born because of causation. Since they are
> born through causation, each phenomenon has no entity.
> Because each phenomenon has no entity, there is in fact no
> coming and no going, no loss and no gain, and therefore this is
> named Shunyata.[6]

Shunyata means "emptiness." No "self-being." We think
there must be a self-being there. Then you can have relations
between the beings, have interactions. After all, the actions
have to be performed *by* beings, don't they? We see this so
strongly that we believe it is impossible to see things otherwise. The suggestion has been made that this is an effect of
our language, which is based on nouns. First you must have
a noun, then you can attach a verb to it, to tell something
about the noun. We don't even have a way of saying "interaction" without implying that there are first beings there
which then interact. But we may be able to understand that
any beings we can conceive of are defined by us in terms of
their relations to one another, especially *contrast* relations,
each one having some quality that others lack. But if each is
thus defined by others, then it does not have its being of itself. Whatever being it has is given it by relations with others.

The challenge to us is that perhaps "entity" isn't a good
category for doing metaphysics—especially practical, experiential metaphysics. But, we may protest, if we are not each
an entity, a being in oneself, who is responsible for our
actions? One answer is: As long as you believe yourself to be
a finite moral agent, you are responsible. There must be
someone to reward or punish, we feel. There must be judg-

ment. This is the foundation of religion. Without this, not only would there be no meaning to life, but people would simply run wild and commit all sorts of crimes. Identifying with the finite ego as moral agent is essential to civilization, to religion, and to any kind of personal satisfaction.

We try to get to unselfishness and compassion without giving up the sense of the self whose nature it is to be selfish. The Buddhist challenge says, If you are interested in good behavior and compassion, then first give up the sense of the ego-self, see that it is unreal; then it will no longer make demands, have cravings, react with anger and violence when its egohood is thwarted. It is contradictory to continue to hold to such an ego-self and at the same time require it to go against its necessary nature, which must be to sustain its proper finitude and self-definition. Real compassion is not an ego-ego relation as anger or envy or desire or grief is. You do not get to compassion while still holding to the entity of the ego-self. See through this idea of "entity," realize that that is a false perception; then compassion will spontaneously arise. But then there will be no one to reward, to enjoy the fruits of this self-sacrificing service to others, no one to be praised and recompensed. True. There will be no ego-personality there to receive the reward. There will only be universal love and compassion. Too bad.

It is a strong challenge, but we may want to search through our tradition again to see if there is any sign that this is what Jesus was trying to tell us—that God is not a judge who metes out eternal rewards and punishments according to the deeds of our short and ignorant lives, but is rather an all-embracing Lover who makes no distinctions among God's Beloved. Perhaps God is even a single Loving Life circulating among all, a God who says, "I am the vine, you are the branches." Perhaps "entity" is a category to be discarded, just as "worthiness" was a category to be discarded—see the Parable of the Workers in the Vineyard—and just as "ranking" was a category to be discarded—see the injunction not to be like the Gentiles' "great men" and its follow-up in the footwashing, which eliminates both "lords" and "servants" in favor of "friends." Perhaps the perfection of God lies in sending sun and rain on good and evil, just and unjust alike, and if we want to be perfect, we must be like that [Mt. 5:45, 48]. No favorites, no preferences. No differences in the Ultimate.

> Sosan Ganchi Zenji says, quoting an ancient Taoist text:
> "The perfect Way knows no difficulties
> Except that it refuses to show preferences; . . .
> To set up what you like against what you dislike—
> This is the disease of the mind.

"Come to me," Jesus calls to those who can hear, "all you who labor and are heavily burdened, and I will give you relief." You don't have to try to give up your ego-adherence as if it were a bad habit and a disvalue—something you "ought not to" do. You simply drop it because you've found out it was a mistake, *not true.* You don't continue to bother with something that's not true. Know the Truth and be free. Come to me and get relief. The Great Relief: No Ego-Entity. Come to me and identify with me rather than with those falsehoods. I am the Reality beyond the appearance of the ego-entity. I am the Way—the Tao—and the Truth and the Life. I am Buddha-Nature. I am in you, and you are in me. There is no Buddha apart from us, no Dharma apart from us. Whatever happens to any one of us, even the least of our kindred, happens to all of us. "I am sitting you, you are sitting me." "In the myriad forms, a single body is revealed."[7]

This "come to me" echoes and re-echoes throughout the Gospel: Come to me, follow me, walk with me, stay with me, stay awake with me, abide in me. But how do we get to "come"? Rinzai says it took him "exhaustive investigation and grinding discipline." Jesus himself admits, "The gate is narrow and the way is hard that leads to life, and those who find it are few" (Matthew 7:14). Essential to this work is close attention to the directive, "Do not judge by appearances, but render a right judgment" (John 7:24). The Noble Eightfold Path of the Buddha begins with Right Views, "right judgment."

So we sit and attend to shifting our understanding from apparent reality to the really real, Eido Roshi says. It is "perhaps the biggest part of our practice as human beings."[8] Once your attention is drawn to the impermanence of the phenomena that appear as if they are entities, your perception of them can alter radically and your sense of identity with them will weaken. You will see your bodily interactions with other bodies and your personality interactions with other personalities, and you will *see* that you are not that. Body and mind will "drop off." In the Hindu idiom, you will be like the bird at the top of the tree who looks on as the lower bird hops about pecking at sweet and sour fruits. In the Christian symbology, the Temple will start to come apart, stone by stone, the structure in which you had been believing and worshiping.

In the beginning, we feel that "we" are practicing, we are getting rid of false ideas, we are gaining insight, we are getting closer to our true self. We may distinguish between "good" meditations and "poor" meditations. "Many of us," says Eido Roshi, "have the mistaken idea that some kind of material body does some kind of spiritual practice. But this idea is a great impediment to practice. . . . It is the spirit that fills the body, not the body that does spiritual practice." "Flesh and blood cannot inherit the kingdom of God, nor does the perishable inherit the imperishable" (1 Corinthians 15:50). "It is the spirit that gives life, the flesh is of no avail" (John 6:63). You may remember also that St. Augustine discovered that the body is in the soul rather than the soul in the body.

But most important is that it is the Holy Spirit that prays in us (cf. Romans 8 :26). "We," as ego-entity, dissolve. That indefinable Something that we noted earlier, "constantly active," which was there before this body-personality and will be hereafter, and yet is Right Here, in, as, this body-personality-appearance—that is praying, meditating, doing spiritual practice. So, really, you should not say "I am Marion and I am doing sitting practice to realize that Something." Rather you should say, "That Something is doing Marion-practice!"[9] Those of you who have read *Zen in the Art of Archery* will remember that "It shoots"; the archer must abandon the perception, the feeling, the idea that the archer shoots. When that notion is released, then It shoots and hits the mark.

Now I want to share with you a couple of stories of people who have had the experience of realizing the Something. The first is from the account of the Chinese Master Han Shan—I don't know of what century. He had been living as a hermit, in silence, with his mind fixed on a single thought, in the context of the teaching: All feelings and sensations arise from one's own mind; they do not come from outside. "One day," he says in his *Autobiography*, "I took a walk." He continues:

> Suddenly I stood still, filled with the realization that I had no body and no mind. All I could see was one great illuminating Whole, omnipresent, perfect, lucid, and serene. It was like an all-embracing mirror from which the mountains and rivers of the earth were projected as reflections. When I awoke from this experience, I felt as "clear-and-transparent" as though my body and mind did not exist at all, whereupon I composed the following stanza:
>
> In a flash, the violent mind stood still;
> Within, without are both transparent and clear.
> After the great somersault
> The great Void is broken through.
> Oh, how freely come and go
> The myriad forms of things!
>
> From then on, both the inward and the outward experience became lucidly clear. Sounds, voices, visions, scenes, forms,

and objects were no longer hindrances. All my former doubts dissolved into nothing. When I returned to my kitchen, I found the cauldron covered with dust. Many days had passed during my experience, of which I, being alone, was unaware.[10]

Let us read an account by another Zen monk, from the *Autobiography of Master Hsüeh Yen:*

[The chief monk, Hsiu said to me], "You should sit erect on your seat, keep your spine straight, make your whole body and mind become one [Hua Tou, or focal point], and pay no attention to drowsiness or wild thoughts." Working in accord with his instructions, I unknowingly forgot both my body and mind—even their very existence. For three days and three nights my mind stayed so serene and clear that I never closed my eyes for a single moment. On the afternoon of the third day I walked through the three gates of the monastery as if I were sitting. Again I came across Hsiu. "What are you doing here?" he asked. "Working on the Tao," I answered. He then said, "What is this you call the Tao?" Not able to answer him, I became more confused and perplexed. With the intention of meditating further I turned back toward the meditation hall. But accidentally I met Hsiu again. He said, "Just open your eyes and see what it is!" After this admonishment I was even more anxious to return to the meditation hall than before. As I was just going to sit down, something broke through abruptly before my face as if the ground were sinking away. I wanted to tell how I felt, but I could not express it. Nothing in this world can be used as a simile to describe it. Immediately I went to find Hsiu. As soon as he saw me he said, "Congratulations!" Holding my hand, he led me out of the monastery. We walked along the river dike, which was full of willow trees. I looked up at the sky and down at the earth. I actually felt that all phenomena and manifestations, the things I saw with my eyes and heard with my ears, the things that disgusted me—including the passion-desires and the blindness—all flowed out from my own bright, true, and marvelous Mind. During the next fortnight no moving phenomena appeared in my mind.[11]

❧ V ❧

Enlightenment and Practice

WE NOW HAVE some notion of what is meant by ceasing to identify with the passing forms of the world. When our desires based on that sense of identity have "gone out" like a candle that has burned down and has no more wax, then we are in *nirvana*. As a meditation state, it corresponds to what Zen layman Katsuki Sekida calls "absolute samadhi"; among the Ox-Herding Pictures, it is number 8, the Empty Circle—no ox, no one seeking or finding the ox, no one at all. We have escaped from, or transcended, or realized the insubstantiality of, the world of impermanent coming and going, interrelating processes, desires chasing one another, karma linkages leading from past to future, concepts describing contrasts: what is called *samsara*. This is Enlightenment.

Now we are ready to begin spiritual life! Some Buddhist schools hold that there are as many as fifty-two further stages through which the *enlightened* person has to pass to reach the maturity of the Buddha! This is where we learn to see how samsara, the world-web of processes, is not different from nirvana and how compassion matches wisdom. To give a very sketchy idea of what goes on here, I will use one version of "Tozan's Five Ranks," as set forth by Katsuki Sekida in his book *Zen Training*.[1] Tozan was a famous Zen master of the eighth and ninth centuries.

The first rank is the Ox-Herding Picture, number 8, Emptiness. This has to be attained in order to know what we truly are and not be deceived. However, if we settle down in this empty, thoughtless condition, our spiritual development will come to an end. So we must return to the world and live in what Sekida, who is a twentieth-century man, calls "positive samadhi," as distinct from "absolute samadhi," contentless consciousness. To describe the way these two aspects of Reality, the absolute and the positive, are integrated, Tozan uses the words *Sho* and *Hen*. Sho means absolute, interior, unity, reality; Hen means relative, exterior, differentiation, appearance. Thus the first rank is called "Hen in Sho" and means that the relative has been completely absorbed into the absolute. In Christian symbology this might translate as the withdrawal of the Word back into the Father, the Emptiness that we symbolize by the nothingness of Holy Saturday, with its stripped altars and vacant tabernacles and lack of ceremony.

In the second rank, we come back from absolute samadhi. We again perceive the relative world, but now we know that the absolute is what is at the heart of it. The second rank is called "Sho in Hen." In the Christian vocabulary, this means that the liberating spiritual death is not the end of the path of growth. It must be followed by resurrection, the return to embodied life, which itself is a developmental state. We may notice that Jesus said to Mary Magdalene, "Do not cling to me—this state of my being—for I have not yet ascended to my Father." And even ascension is not the end, either, as we will see as we go through the ranks. But here, in the second rank, resurrection, we experience unity in differentiation, we see the Absolute in every differentiated being. This makes all things appear glorious and intimately related to one another. No need, after all, to leave the world to find Buddha-Reality.

All this *is* Buddha. Everything is close and familiar, nothing extraordinary. We see phenomena, and that is quite all right.

The third rank is concerned with putting these two—the first and second ranks—together so that they mutually indwell one another. It is called "Coming from Sho," coming from absolute samadhi to positive samadhi. This is the foundation for spiritual life, the state in which to abide for ordinary daily life. I might mention that Ramakrishna also pointed out this state, the coming back into ordinary consciousness from the absolute unity and formlessness of samadhi. In his tradition this state is called *Bhavamukha*, and in the symbology of his spiritual life, he heard Divine Mother tell him: "Remain in *Bhavamukha*." That means, "Do not limit yourself to the *Nirguna*—the formless—aspect, but be also the *Saguna*—with form—aspect. For you are the Whole Reality, both with form and without form." Just at the moment of "coming back," from deep samadhi, "Coming from Sho," you find yourself on the frontier, on what we might call the "interface." Stay there, he was told. We might say he was told, "Be true God and true man."

We can also interpret the Christian concepts of the Father and the Son in such a way. The Father would be the absolute, the formless, the invisible; and the Son would be the relative, the world of forms, the visible, the incarnate. An interesting text, John 1:18, says: "No one has ever seen God; the only-begotten God, who is in the bosom of the Father, That One manifested him." There are several points here. First, the Father is invisible; never seen, not because we can't *see* but because the Father can't be *seen*. But there is an offspring of this invisible One, the *monogēnes theos*, the singly generated God —it can be read either as the only offspring or as the offspring of only one parent (the word originally meant "born of one mother"). This Offspring God is said to be in the "bosom" (*kolpon* in Greek) of the Father, the big pocket of one's upper garment in which, for instance, a shepherd can carry a lamb. The word literally means "hollow," and we right away remember "Empty—Emptiness." The Offspring God dwells in the Emptiness of the Invisible God. And That One "exegetes." That's the word, and it means to reveal and interpret the sacred mysteries. Here we have clearly the manifest and visible *coming out of* but also *remaining in* the unmanifest and the invisible. Later in John's Gospel we find "I am in the Father and the Father is in me." In Zen language, Hen is in Sho, and Sho is in Hen; the relative is in the absolute, and the formless is in the forms. John also says that the Son "comes from" the Father: "I came from the Father and have come into the world; again, I am leaving the world and going to the Father" (John 16:28).

Tozan's text says of this rank, "The Way is found in the Emptiness. You have the universe under your sway." Ramakrishna puts it this way: "All that appears in the world passes through you, issues from you. The Supreme Self engages in its divine play through you and as you." John says of the Exegeting God, "All things were generated through him," and the Epistle to the Colossians says, "He is the image of the Invisible God, the firstborn of all creation; for in him all things were created, in heaven and on earth . . . all things were created through him and for him. He is before all things, and in him all things hold together." And Jesus himself declares: "All things have been delivered to me by my Father, and no one fully knows the Son except the Father, and no one fully knows the Father except the Son" (Matthew 11:27).

This mutual indwelling of Hen in Sho and Sho in Hen, says Tozan, is the full reality of our life; this is what we strive to realize: full knowledge of Hen by our life in Sho, and full knowledge of Sho by our life in Hen. Perhaps in our liturgical imagery we can liken it to the Feast of Pentecost, the celebration of the Holy Spirit. The Holy Spirit is the Bond of Unity of the Invisible Father and the Exegeting Son. It is the Integration and Expression of "God's varied grace," as the First Letter of Peter has it; it is the One Spirit with its diverse gifts, the One Spirit whose speech is heard in all languages—think of animal, plant, and mineral languages, of electromagnetic and gravitation languages, as well as of music and body language. It is the Spirit who is the Vivificator, the Life-Maker. Outflowing life starts from here. In our liturgical cycle, it takes half a year to reach this point, and half a year to go on from here. This is Tozan's third rank.

And now Tozan gives insights into how to go on. He sets up two more ranks, which presume this perfect integration of Sho and Hen. In the fourth rank, called "Perfection in Hen," one spontaneously shows Enlightenment in every action, "like a lotus flower shining in the fire." Such a person, capable of revealing the Invisible, can also enter into the experience of others, thinking and feeling with them. This is compassion, feeling together with. The world of Hen is now clear and distinct, experienced vividly in every detail, but every item in it is Buddha, and they all interpenetrate each other. Are we reminded of "Whatever happens to any one of these my kindred happens to me"? If it is the case that "The Father is in me and I am in the Father," and "I am in you and you are in me," then does it not follow that each of us is also "in" every other? A vast cosmic mutual indwelling? A gigantic Holy Communion? "Feed one another as I have fed you"? The Feast of the Holy Trinity has its near reflection in the Feast of Corpus Christi, followed by the Feast of the Sacred Heart, the divine Generosity for both giving and receiving all the forms of the world.

When the fifth rank is reached, "Perfection in Integration," everything is complete and one becomes totally natural, thoroughly integrated and entirely devoted to the salvation of all. Perhaps this is the culmination of the mysteries in the Feast of the Assumption. In the Zen tradition there are several images for this state. One is the old person sitting quietly by the fire, uniting all that exists. Another is the Tenth Ox-Herding picture, a jolly person returning to the village with gifts for the villagers. A third is someone who continues to do good to one who is doing wrong things; such a person perseveres in kindness to help the other find joy in truth—like a shepherd who does not give up until the lost sheep is found and rescued, like the God who sends sun and rain on the good and evil alike. A Zen koan asks, "When you think neither of good nor of evil, at that very moment, what is your Original Face?" Prior to nourishing yourself on the fruit of knowledge according to Good and Evil, who are you? Right now, at a level prior to that way of experiencing and assessing the world, who are you? What is your Original Face? Let us say one face is your pure existence in absolute samadhi. And another is your unending cultivation of Holy Buddha-hood after enlightenment, positive samadhi in ordinary daily life (pp. 237–52). Two faces, one looking out through the other, One Face. Interface.

We can develop this theme a little further. The *Engaku Sutra* says, "When you sit, do not seek for enlightenment. Do not try to push away the world of defilement. If you have delusions, do not try to extinguish them." Strange doctrine! We thought that was just what we *were* supposed to do. Enlightenment is good, delusion is bad. But that was only the first level of understanding; now we are going deeper. Even "delusion" is no other than the manifestation of Buddha-Nature. Both defilement and purity are none other than the Universal Reality. And anyway, we are no longer assessing experiences as good or evil. "The perfect Way refuses to make distinctions." Sun and rain on the good and the evil alike. You want to be perfect? Be like that (Sermon on the Mount). Don't play favorites with your experiences, don't have preferences. The *Bhagavad Gita* says:

> One to me is fame and shame,
> One to me is loss and gain,
> One to me is pleasure, pain.

We have just learned that we are *not* the phenomena. Now we hear that we must consent to *be* phenomena too. Don't cling to being God. Be willing to empty yourself and take on form, even the form of a servant, and to be born in the likeness of a human being. And being in that human form, be willing to humble yourself and become obedient unto death, even death on a cross (Philippians 2:7). No preferences.

The *Heart Sutra of the Perfection of Wisdom* is said to contain the essence of the entire Mahayana teaching, especially in the first two sentences:

> Form is not different from Emptiness,
> And Emptiness is not different from form.
> Form is Emptiness and Emptiness is form.

Garma Chang, now teaching at Pennsylvania State University, in his *Buddhist Teaching of Totality*,[2] comments that here we see a basic difference between two views: one possibility is to say that the appearance of form is total delusion, unreal, and to be got rid of; the other says that the forms are not to be destroyed, are not to be resisted or despised, are not unreal. On the contrary, the very realization of the identity of the world of forms and the absolute Emptiness is what brings forth enlightenment and liberation. This latter is the Mahayana view.

Chang further remarks that discussions of these opening lines of the *Heart Sutra* usually focus on the first clause: "Form is Emptiness," which we also have treated with some emphasis to make clear how essential it is to abandon identifying ourselves with our descriptions. But seldom, says Chang, is the deeper aspect, "Emptiness is Form," thoroughly examined. Christians who want to see what can be learned from the East may want to look into this, to see if, in spite of its strong difference from the typical Christian personal-entity-relationship view, any insight is provoked in us on hearing about this Mahayanist view.

To see if we can get some further light on how "Emptiness

is Form," I turn to the thirteenth-century Japanese Zen Master Dōgen. Dōgen went to China to learn Zen, and he took with him a very natural problem. Why, he wanted to know, do we need to practice, if—as our religion teaches us—we are all already enlightened? I suggest that the answer he discovered can be seen as the working out of this "Emptiness is Form." His view has been called "Mystical Realism," and it was quite revolutionary in its day. This is how I understand it. Dōgen all the time relates Enlightenment to Practice and Practice to Enlightenment. I think these are his terms for Emptiness and Form, or Sho and Hen. They are the double aspect of the nondual Reality. As for the answer to his question, the first answer is the obvious one: we have to practice because we do not yet realize that we are by nature Buddha. But the more interesting answer, and the one that pertains to our question, is that we still practice because "Emptiness is Form." That is to say, *we* practice because *Emptiness itself practices.* That is How It Is—with capital letters.

Here is a story. One warm day a Zen Teacher was employing a hand fan, when a monastic came and asked: "The nature of the wind is abiding and universally present. Why do you still use your fan?" The Teacher's answer was: "You know only the nature of the wind as abiding; you do not yet know the truth of its being universally present." The monastic said: "What is the truth of its being universally present?" Without a word, the Teacher continued fanning. The monastic recognized the truth and bowed.[3]

The wind is said to be both "abiding" and "universally present." Fanning may not be necessary for the "abiding" aspect—Enlightenment, Emptiness, absolute samadhi, Sho —but it is necessary for the realization of the "universally present" aspect—Practice, Form, positive samadhi, Hen. And the Full Reality requires both. No Hen without Sho, but also no Sho without Hen.

Hee-jin Kim, in his exposition of Dōgen as mystical realist, gives this explanation of the story: "The nature of the wind is such that it cannot be conceptualized or contemplated but is instead to be actualized; furthermore, it is not potentiality being actualized, but rather actuality creating itself through the act of fanning. . . . Only when we create our own identity through our body and mind, only then does Buddha-nature create itself." "The self-creation of Buddha-nature itself constitutes all the phenomena of the universe."[4]

We also have a Gospel story in which the wind figures as a symbol for Ultimate Reality. In explanation of his assertion that to see the Kingdom of God, one must have been born from above, from Spirit, Jesus says to Nicodemus: "The wind blows where it will and you hear it, but you don't know where it comes from or where it goes. It is like this with everyone who is born of the Spirit" (John 3). Invisibility, freedom, no origin, no destiny, essentially dynamic. Now add: can't be conceptualized or viewed but only actualized, actualized as *actuality* creating itself. "That which is born of the Spirit *is* spirit." That's what it's like with everyone who is born of the Spirit. And everyone *is*, we just don't know it. And even when we do know it, we go on actualizing Actuality. The exegeting Offspring God is just as much God as the Invisible God is. This is the nature of the dynamic God, the Living God. Do you begin to get some sense of how "Emptiness is Form"?

In Dōgen's Zen, Practice and Enlightenment are one; they are not related as means to end. They remain distinct, yet they are the same Reality. Doesn't this sound like the Athanasian Creed? The Father is not the Son and the Son is not the Father; yet they are not two Gods but one God. And the practical consequence is that perfect religion is caring for the widows and orphans and everything else that you do in daily life. Therefore all is to be done with the same mind as sitting meditation is done. For there is no difference. It is all Practice, and Practice is Enlightenment.

In introducing this doctrine, I spoke as though there was practice before enlightenment in order to attain knowledge of Enlightenment, and then continued practice after enlightenment, because Enlightenment itself practices. Now I have to say that there is no "after" and no "before" enlightenment. Enlightenment is eternal; even when Enlightenment is Practice—when Emptiness *is* Form—Enlightenment always *is*. You are always in Enlightenment and always in Practice. Therefore, a Dōgen teacher, in giving instruction for practice, advises the disciples not to seek enlightenment beyond practice, for practice itself is Original Enlightenment.

> Because it is already enlightenment of practice, there is no end to enlightenment; because it is already practice of enlightenment, there is no beginning to practice.[5]

I read that this way: The reality is, on the one hand, the enlightenment that comes through practice, is experienced in practice, as practice. There is no end to practice, and therefore there is no end to enlightenment. On the other hand, the Reality is Enlightenment's own Practice, and there is no beginning for Enlightenment, so no beginning for Practice. The Total Real is Practice's Enlightenment and Enlightenment's Practice. Form is Emptiness and Emptiness is Form.

This is what Dōgen calls "ongoing enlightenment," Even when you first begin to practice, it is already Enlightenment-as-you that is practicing. You are never anything other than, or separate from, Buddha-nature, Emptiness, Enlightenment, Absolute Reality. And you are never not-practicing. Enlightenment does not "transcend" the world of relative, finite beings. Enlightenment is *realized in* that world. Emptiness "blooms" as Form. The experiences of the finite world are not illusions but the "flowers of Emptiness." All natural beings, in their myriad forms and processive interactions, coming into being and perishing, are characterized by Dōgen as "the whole body of Emptiness leaping out of itself."[6] Shall we say the child of God is the Invisible God giving birth to Itself?

Dōgen uses another metaphor. "It is possible," he says, "to realize and penetrate into the *inaudible in speech*. Unless you attain *ongoing enlightenment* [this enlightenment-as-practice], you do not experience it; if it is not speech [but only the Inaudible], you do not verify it in your subjectivity. It is neither manifestation nor hiddenness (John 1:18 said it is both, which is almost the same thing). . . . Accordingly, when speech [the Word] is *realized* [actually spoken], this itself *is* Ongoing Enlightenment" [*Shobogenzo*, "Bukkojoji"]. We realize that the Inaudible resides in the audible itself, just as the audible is nothing but the Inaudible made available. This "speech" is not trapped in a dualism of the audible and the inaudible.

Is this the secret of the Divine Word, the Word that carries the necessary silence of the Inaudible, the Invisible God, with it, the Word through which the Inaudible speaks, the Word which *is* the inaudible *speaking*? When the Samaritan woman presses Jesus to see whether he can go beyond the category of "Messiah," he answers, "I AM—the one speaking," the "speaking aspect" or "speaking version" of the I AM, the Exegete, the Audible that is one with the Inaudible. Where is the sense in asking for the Inaudible, as if it were something separate from and beyond the Audible? Jesus says to Philip, "What do you mean, Show us the Father?" Whoever hears the Audible *is hearing* the Inaudible. It is when Speech is *realized* that Ongoing Enlightenment is present.[7]

Like Dōgen, we may be in Great Doubt about the relation of Practice and Enlightenment. If Enlightenment is the whole Truth, what is the meaning of Practice? In the world of Practice, beings are born and pass away. Where is Enlightenment then? Until we experience it ourselves, we do not believe; we don't see how it is. It's either the coming and going of meaningless words or else eternal silence. Until we experience it as Speech, we cannot "verify it in our own subjectivity." We are like the apostle called "Doubting Thomas" confronted with the report of the resurrection of Jesus. But then Thomas had his own experience, verified it in his own subjectivity. What did he see? Perhaps he *saw* —realized— the coincidence of Practice and Enlightenment. Perhaps he *saw* the union of the mortal and the immortal. He saw the body that had died, with characteristics that he knew. And he saw a body that could do things no mortal body could do (appear suddenly within a locked room). And he *saw* them *together* as *one body*—one body, which invited him into intimacy with itself, urged him to verify in his own subjective experience the truth of its reality. Did Thomas see then that Practice doesn't lead to or point to, symbolize or represent, Enlightenment, but *is* Enlightenment leaping out of itself? Is it this nondual copresence of the Invisible and the Exegete, Silence and the Word, that is his "Lord and God," that is the Total Real?

This is what Dōgen calls "the koan realized in life," the event in which Buddha-nature is revealed, its Real Presence made manifest. Present living and lived realities of everyday life are the realizations of Truth itself. What is Reality? What is Truth? Just This! Whatever it is, as-it-is, as-it-is-ing. That's It. What is this? Just This! I AM—Speaking Version![8]

Let us conclude with a poem by Abhishiktananda:

> In this world, out of this world,
> seer of what is beyond sight,
> we go secretly and hidden, unknown,
> mad with the madness of those who know,
> free with the freedom of the Spirit,
> filled with essential bliss,
> established in the mystery of the non-dual,
> free from all sense of otherness,
> our hearts filled with the unique experience of the Self,
> fully and for ever awake. . . .[9]

∽ VI ∽

Gospel Zen

"**W**HAT IS YOUR PRACTICE?" That's a Zen question. You don't hear Christians ask that kind of question very often. They're more apt to say, "What do you believe?" or even just, "What church do you go to?"

Typical answers to the Zen question are: "My practice is just sitting." "I am counting my breaths." "My koan is *Mu.*" "I am giving full attention to each thing I do." "I am intensely asking myself, 'What is my real nature?'"

How would we answer such a question on "practice" from the Gospel? It might be interesting to try. Traditional Christian teaching has told us what to believe (or "hold") about doctrine, what to do in the way of receiving sacraments, how to live a moral life and follow the customs of the church. But we haven't usually been offered a *method* for self-realization, for reaching illumination, for attaining salvation, comparable to those suggested above. Perhaps we think that the Gospel doesn't deal in "methods" but instead demands faith. But even the *faith* of the Gospel is a kind of method and can be cultivated, as we shall see. I think there may indeed be quite a lot of advice about "practice" in the Gospel, and if we look for it with this in mind, we may be surprised at what we find.

I propose to make a small raid on this rich treasury by

looking in the New Testament for instructions on what to do, interwoven with comments on "how things are" and "what to expect." I ignore the usual or even the obvious meaning, but I hope I can plead that I am using the New Testament in an "accommodated" sense. Along the way I will also drop in an occasional remark from a Buddhist source to help highlight the interpretation I am suggesting.

Where does practice begin? The moral life is, of course, absolutely prerequisite. Both Buddhism and Christianity recognize this. Mahayana's ten cardinal precepts prohibit: (1) the taking of life, (2) theft, (3) unchastity, (4) lying, (5) drinking or encouraging others to drink alcoholic liquor, (6) speaking of the misdeeds of others, (7) praising oneself and reviling others, (8) giving spiritual or material aid grudgingly, (9) anger, and (10) blaspheming the Three Treasures (the Buddha, the Teachings, and the Community, as One, as Manifested, and as Preserved). Other lists add using immoral language, gossiping, coveting, holding wrong views, and destroying the harmony of the community.[1]

But there is a sense in which these are preliminary to the direct assault on the mystery of life, as is also evident in the New Testament story of the rich young man who asks Jesus what he must do to have eternal life. Jesus told him to keep the commandments and, when pressed, enumerated them for him: You shall not kill, commit adultery, steal, or bear false witness. You shall honor your parents and love your neighbor as yourself. The young man replied that he had been observing all these and inquired what he still lacked. At that point the serious commitment was broached: Jesus said to him, "If you would be perfect, go, sell what you possess and give to the poor . . . and come, follow me" (Matthew 19:20–21). Follow me into the heart of the mystery.

If the rich young man had followed Jesus, what would he have been instructed to do next? Two verses occur to me, Mark 6:31 and Matthew 6:6:

Come away by yourselves to a lonely place, and rest a while.
(For many were coming and going and they had no leisure.)

When you pray, go into your room and shut the door, and
pray to your Father in private.

Our lives are usually characterized by "many comings and
goings" and "no leisure." So the first thing we have to do is
"come away by ourselves to a place where we can be alone."
The fact that many people find even this first step almost
impossible to take is a fearful commentary on our culture, its
values, and its lifestyle. It is ironic that if I wish to practice
meditation to gain self-knowledge, strength of character, and
insight into reality, I must have, to begin with, sufficient
insight, self-knowledge, and strength to realize that meditation is important, that I myself need it, and want it enough to
make me contend against all the forces in my environment
that would impede me. This is why people resort to going to
special places to practice meditation. Institutionalizing it
seems to make it acceptable in a way that just doing it at
home by oneself isn't.

Having reached a lonely place, the first thing most of us
have to do is, literally, "rest a while." Catch our breath. Shift
gears. Let go the concerns of the busy place. Turn our attention toward the great questions of life: What is this life of
ours all about? Why are we here? What kind of being are we?
Can we cease to exist? What is the meaning and value of our
life? What is the vast cosmos? How is it that we can know it?
What is consciousness? What is it in me that knows, and
knows that it knows that it knows? What is my deepest
nature?

Asking these questions is "going into your private room."
We have to turn the mind inward, away from particular
problems and issues of the moment. *Really asking* such questions is "praying." We ask them "in secret." This means that
they are personal, private questions, not public or social

questions. The question is not, What does my culture, tradition, church, family, believe about this? Rather, What do *I*
believe, in secret. And not just, What do I believe? but *What is*
true?

Whom do we ask? The Gospel says to ask "your Father." I
propose that we interpret this as meaning "seek your
Source," the Source of your being. And this helps us understand why we have to go apart, go into the private room, and
ask in secret—because the Source of my being is to be found
only in my inmost self.

In earlier translations of the New Testament, this verse
read, "Go into your closet." This used to call up puzzling
images for children, who were used to "closets" as small
compartments for hanging clothes. I had this image myself,
and I remember noticing with interest that Amy, in *Little*
Women, had thought the same thing; she had taken it literally, removed the clothes, and made a tiny prayer room of
her closet. More recently, an adult friend who was living in
cramped quarters did the same thing. In this sophisticated
age, when so many people are talking about coming *out* of
one closet or another, here are some of us trying to get *into*
the closet.

So, "Go into your closet." But what is my closet? This
brings us to the first problem, which is also the last problem:
What is my inmost self, my true nature, and how do I enter
it?

Another name for the "inmost self" is "heart." in the Sermon on the Mount, we read, "Where your treasure is, there
will your heart be also" (Matthew 6:21). So a clue to finding
the inmost self, or heart, is to look for the treasure. This
means, look for what we value. To value something with
your consciousness means to pay attention to it, to have a lot
of thoughts and feelings about it. Attention, thoughts, and
feelings are the money, the currency, of consciousness.

Something that is worth a lot of attention, thought, and feeling is a consciousness-treasure.

That doesn't mean that the "treasure" is necessarily something we like, something we find pleasant or desirable. It may be quite the contrary. There is another verse that says, "Where the carcass is, there will the vultures be gathered together" (Luke 17:37). Our attention, thoughts, and feelings may be clustered around something painful. A lot of our consciousness-energy may be invested in suffering. Nevertheless, this is still a clue to where our "heart" is. "Where you experience suffering, you can also find freedom from suffering," says Achaan Chah.[2]

We often try to dull our suffering or divert ourselves from it. If we persist in this practice, we will remain blind, and the suffering won't go away, either (cf. Matthew 13:14–15). If, instead, we go *into* it, we will begin to ask the great questions. What is it in me that is suffering? Why is it suffering? Where does this suffering come from? Such questions lead us into our "heart," into our "closet."

What is our consciousness? How does it work? What produces the effect of suffering?

Any suffering is a perception of a threat to our life on some level. The level may be biological life or emotional life. It may be a threat to our health, or a threat to our dignity. Basically, the threat is against whatever we consider to be our "self." We naturally try to preserve our "self" in the face of such threats. But the Gospel says that it is precisely such attempts at preservation that make the threats even worse: "Whoever seeks to gain his life will lose it, but whoever loses his life will preserve it" (Luke 17:33; this appears in each of the Gospels, in some of them twice). *There* is a Zen koan for you! What is the meaning of this saying? What is meant by "his life" in each case? What is "gain"? "lose"? "preserve"? What is really the *life*? *Whose* is it?

Struggling with these questions, we are led back into self-search. What is my true life? Here in my heart, in my private world, where the suffering is, is where some kind of mistake is being made. Perhaps the life I'm trying to save isn't my true life at all, and all my efforts to shore it up only cause me to go further away (in realization) from my true life. Whereas, if I could let go of this apparent life, I might find my true life. Jesus warned, "Don't judge by appearances, but render a true judgment" (John 7:24).

Stimulated by our question and encouraged by the words of the Teacher, we throw ourselves wholly into the search for the true self. We "leave everything" (Mark 10:28) in the sense that this search for the true self now receives top priority in our life, and we "follow" the track pointed out by the Teacher. The true self becomes to us a hoard of gold buried in a field, or a single pearl of inestimable value, for whose sake we are willing to "sell" everything else (Matthew 13:44–45). That is, we organize and evaluate everything else in our life in terms of whether and how it helps us in our *practice*, in our quest for the true self. If we have a job to do, we do it in such a way as to help us with our quest. If we have a family to care for, we put our heart into it as a way to find our true self. We "seek first the Kingdom of Heaven" (Matthew 6:33).

Singleness of purpose now characterizes us. We have been "busy and troubled about many things." Now we see that "only one thing is really necessary" (Luke 10:41–42). We must focus ourselves onto one overwhelming purpose and seek enlightenment: "If your eye is single, your whole body will be filled with light" (Matthew 6:22). This singleness is an important clue. The Greek word is *haplous*; it means "one-fold, single, all in one way, not compound or double, absolute." Not only the purpose of our life should be single, the mind itself, the "eye" must become single, not double. The look, the attending, the thinking and feeling, must not double themselves.

But usually, of course, we do double our minds, just as we

usually seek to save our lives. The lives that we seek to save are relative lives, in commerce with the rest of the earthly environment or in social relations with the community. These are realities, and healthful properties in them are desirable on their own levels, but mistaking them for the true self is what causes the suffering, because these relational processes are by nature, and inevitably, changeable.

In fact, they are constantly changing. They are processes, simply a flow of changes. The chemicals of which the cells of our bodies are made do not remain the same for long but are broken down and eliminated, their places being taken by new molecules. And in many tissues, the cells themselves live for only a few days and are then replaced. So living consists of a continuous death and rebirth.[3]

It is the same with our thoughts and feelings. Trying to arrest this flow of life and cling to some particular arrangement, or ward off some unfavorable arrangement, is contrary to the nature of this level of reality, in which all things change and pass and come again. We have to understand that "the form of this world is passing away" (1 Corinthians 7:31). Not only does the form pass, but "passing away" is what the "form" *is: change* is the name of the game.

Therefore, we cannot hold this world or any particular experience, cannot cling to it. Setting our will against this fact of reality is what causes our suffering. When we see this, really *see* it for ourselves, as it applies to every concrete instance in our own personal life, then we will be "close to the Kingdom of Heaven." We must reconcile ourselves to this fact and turn ourselves to what does endure. "Do not labor for the food which perishes, but for the food which endures to eternal life" (John 6:27).

> Do not lay up for yourselves treasures on earth, where moth and rust consume and where thieves break in and steal, but lay up for yourself treasures in heaven, where neither moth nor rust consumes and where thieves do not break in and steal. (Matthew 6:19–20)

Now, the doubling of the mind—of the attention, thoughts, and feelings—is similar to this mistake of clinging to the changing. What changes is necessarily relational, relative, not absolute. The world of the relative *has* to be multiple (so that there can always be *others* to which one can "relate"), therefore, not single. The doubling of the mind is also relational. It consists of comparisons, contrasts, criticisms, and comments. There is one mind, so to speak, that is actually engaging the world, doing things, and then there is a second mind, sitting on the sidelines, making remarks. It is with this second mind that we usually talk to ourselves, inside our heads. We tell ourselves what to do, comment on how well we're doing it, wonder what other people think of how we're doing it, how our behavior compares with the norms of our culture, and so on. It is this second mind that, in this way, builds up what we call our self-image. And, of course, it is in this self-image that a great deal of our suffering is located.

The second mind is very relational in its operations. It never actually unites itself with an object; in fact, by acting as a kind of middleman between the genuine agent and the object, it impedes the action and is a barrier between the subject and the object. It deflects attention, drains off energy, and frequently sets up conflicting thoughts and feelings about what is going on.

It constantly talks about whatever is going on, and passes judgment on it by comparing it with other examples, either other people or some ideal standard. It wants approval, honor, respect, and praise from these relational sources, from other people, and from the second mind's own judgment. All this causes suffering and prevents us from finding our true self. Jesus says, "How can you believe, who receive glory from one another and do not seek the glory that comes from the only [one, single] God?" (John 5:44).

"How can you believe?" he asks. We don't believe. We do the opposite: we doubt. To *doubt* is to *double* the mind. Since this is the "way that leads to destruction," Jesus is urgent in exhorting us to cease doubting. "Have faith in God," he says (Mark 11:22); "Don't be faithless, but believing" (John 20:27). "Where is your faith?" he asks (Luke 8:25); "Why did you doubt?" (Matthew 14:31).

Unfortunately, we have a very narrow view of what is meant by "believing" and "doubting." We think of them both in the context of accepting someone's word for something of which we do not have direct knowledge. Or we think of them in the context of reposing trust and confidence in someone. But perhaps these are not their deepest meanings nor the most helpful in our quest for the true self. I suggest that "doubting" means *doubling the mind*, and "believing" means *keeping the mind single*.

Believing means keeping the mind single. What a strange idea. Yet Matthew 21:21 says: "Have faith and do not doubt." The Greek word for "doubt" here is *diakrithete*. It means, literally, "divide (*krino*) in two (*dia*)." From this literal meaning we derive "distinguish" and "judge," and finally "doubt." But if we are not to divide in two, then we must remain one, maintain unity, wholeness. Remaining one is not doubling, not doubting, but believing. And the singleness of "believing" is tied to the singleness of "the only God" (John 5:44), as we saw above.

At this point I think we should introduce the fundamental law of this (Judeo-Christian) practice, which is "The Lord your God, the Lord is One. And you shall love the Lord your God with your whole heart, your whole mind, your whole soul, and your whole strength" (Matthew 22:37; Mark 12:30, 33; Luke 10:27). These four faculties, or four aspects of human being, can be interpreted in various ways. I have, for instance, called them intellect (mind), will (strength), imagination (soul), and affectivity (heart). But we could also take them as referring to the source of motivation and action (heart); the way we perceive the world (mind); our vital energies, sensitivities, instincts and feelings (soul); and our will to persevere with force of character (strength). And no doubt there are other ways.

Keeping the mind—or, more generally now, the consciousness—single, means keeping our heart whole, keeping our mind whole, our soul and our strength, not letting any of them divide in two. So when we pray, we enter into our private chamber, our own secret consciousness, and we try to find our truest self by unifying and keeping whole our heart, mind, soul, and strength. This unification of the consciousness is what is usually called "concentration": centering together. It is basic to spiritual practice.

How do you do this concentration? You just *be* what you're actually doing at the moment, without thinking/feeling *about* the fact that you're doing it. When you set your hand to the plow, you just concentrate on plowing and go straight ahead without looking back to see what you plowed, or how well you plowed (Luke 9:62).

You put your whole mind onto plowing, the *activity*, in the moment in which you are actually doing it. You don't allow the mind to divide into two, half on *plowing* and half on *plowed*. You notice the plow, the field, whatever you have to attend to in order to plow straight, and merge your whole mind into the objective reality of these things in order that the plowing may be done correctly. And in fact, if you can put your whole mind on the activity, not dividing some part to look back and see what you *have plowed*, you will cut a beautiful furrow.

You put your whole will into plowing. You do not divide your will in two by partly consenting to plow, and partly resenting and resisting it and wishing you were doing something else. You "give yourself to" this activity totally, *as* you do it. The act of plowing and the act of willing to plow become the same thing.

Similarly, you do not allow your imagination to conjure up

some other scene for you to enjoy in daydreaming while you plod behind your plow. The imagination must coincide with the perception of present reality and "be here now." *This* is where you actually are, this is reality. Don't create a fantasy and divide your consciousness between where you really are and where you aren't. Know who you are and where you are and what you are doing and really *be* there.

Finally, put all your feelings into this plowing because this is where your life is at this moment. You have no other life here and now except this plowing. Therefore feel this plowing thoroughly, feel it in every way you can. Feel it through your body with all your senses, with your emotions, your aesthetic sense, your sense of satisfaction with work—whatever feelings are appropriate, unify them here and merge them into the act of plowing. *Become plowing.* This is *you* at this moment. This is where you really are and what you are really doing.

That's how you center yourself, how you "concentrate." All those perceptions, feelings, thoughts, wills, energies, all of them center in the present act, in the center of *you*. *You* are the actor, you are the one who is plowing. If you practice this, you will "center" in the center of yourself. You will be in your "inner chamber," and you will be aware that life is gushing up in you at that point (John 7:38), that your being is being sustained from moment to moment. You are in immediate contact with your Source. How intense is this act of living! How vibrant and full! This is not-doubting, keeping the consciousness single. And sure enough, when this "eye" is single, the whole body is filled with light.

Another way of putting this is that we have to stop judging. "Don't divide (your mind) in two" also means "don't judge." And another scripture says explicitly, "Judge not, that you be not judged" (Matthew 7:1). The whole issue of judging is a very interesting one and can be developed at greater length, especially in connection with theories about original sin. In this context, nourishing ourselves on the good/evil dichotomy is the original or fundamental mistake on which all other faults and sufferings are based.

There are, of course, many kinds of judging; in fact, most of life is made up of acts of selection, or choice, or judging.[4] We are not being told not to judge whether it's going to rain today, or whether this vegetable is fresh, or which dentist to employ, or what career to take up, or what candidate to vote for, or what verdict to render in a court of law. Obviously, life is full of judgments of these types.

It's not only human beings who make judgments. All creation does it. What holds the finite universe in existence and enables it to evolve is constant distinction and preference. Symmetry-breaking, it is called, abolishing reversibility and ambiguity by electing one possibility out of a field of possibilities.[5]

But the ground of finitude is the nonfinite. And since finitude is made by distinction and contrast, by mutually limited beings, the nonfinite is precisely that in which there is no distinction or contrast or limitation (John 1:17). It is this nonfinite or noncontrasting ground that is indicated when we speak of the true self.

What we are trying to do in meditation (Zen) is to realize that we are this ground, as well as the finite expressions of it with which we are more familiar. God is the Ground of the whole universe and, as such, is impartial (Deuteronomy 10:27), perfectly symmetrical. And there is something in us that is the image of this Ground, if indeed we are not rooted in that one Ground itself (Matthew 5:48). That is what we are trying to find, and that is why, when we are trying to find it, *we must leave off judging.* Once we have found it and thoroughly realized our root in it, centered ourselves in it, then we can freely express ourselves in the finite in creative ways, "enter the city with helping hands."[6]

When we stop judging, we become complete or perfect.

This means unified or symmetrical. It is practiced by being impartial. Jesus points to this when he says that God sends rain and sunshine on everyone equally, regardless of whether they're good or evil, and we should be like that (Matthew 5:43–48). We can apply this not only to moral relations with other people in daily life but to meditation practice and what goes on in our own heads, in our private chamber when we are trying to reach our Source.

When we sit in meditation, we see that all our internal or emotional life consists of making judgments. We are always evaluating our subjective experiences with respect to whether they are pleasant or painful. We distinguish what happens to us according to whether it is advantageous or disadvantageous. We look at everything in terms of our desires and aversions, our hopes and fears. We're not content just to *have* the experience, we also have to pass judgment on whether it was a good experience or an evil experience.

The trouble with this kind of judgment is that it goes beyond its data. The data will indicate whether an event was advantageous or the reverse for some particular being in some particular context with respect to some particular standard of judgment—all completely *relative*. But when we make our emotional judgment on our experience, we absolutize the value. It becomes totally, or without qualification, good or evil. And it's good or evil not for the body or the career or the emotions or the situation, but, again, without qualifications, for me as a whole. This means that I am *identifying myself* with what happens to the relative aspects of myself, as though these were all there is to me. This is the mistake, this is why such judging prevents us from centering ourselves in our *complete* self.

All these things that can be good or evil for us in one respect or another are changeable things. If we set our hearts on them, we will have no security (Matthew 6:19–20). That is to say, further, we will have *no reality*; for the changing, the contrasting, the partial, the particular, have to be rooted in a ground that sustains all particulars and therefore *is not any particular self*. All forms depend on the formless. If we want to find our true self, find our Source, we must find this formless Ground, the impartial, the complete.

If I say of anything I experience, "This is good," it is equivalent to saying, "Give it to me; let me keep it." If I say, "This is evil," it is equivalent to saying, "Take it away." But "The Lord gives and the Lord takes away; blessed be the name of the Lord." That was the attitude of Job (see Job 1:21), and it is the only realistic attitude to take. To believe that we—the real we, the complete we, not just this or that particular and relative aspect of ourselves—*have to* avoid certain things is to fail to know the truth about ourselves.

The better thing to do is to be neutral about the experiences, not to judge them in an absolute way, but to call them correctly in their own relative contexts and take appropriate action with respect to them in those contexts. If it is pleasant, I thoroughly recognize it as pleasant. If it is distasteful, I thoroughly admit it is distasteful. Then I forget about its being pleasant or distasteful and just go straight ahead.

This is what we learn how to do in the secret place of meditation. As we withdraw from judging our experiences and simply observe them, noting objectively how they relate in their relative ways to their particular contexts, we also realize that *we* who are doing the observing are not dependent on these experiences. *We* are not helped or hindered by them. We are quite impartial with respect to them. Not only are we not dependent on them; *they* are dependent on *us*. All these experiences "live and move and have their being" in us. *We ourselves are the ground of their relative reality.*

So if we can let go of evaluating and taking sides, simply accepting our experiences impartially, our consciousness will gradually center itself in this ground of completeness and wholeness, "a state of pure 'Beingness' without any differentiation; that is, one is no longer this or that (i.e., anything in particular), neither a body nor a mind. . . . One is that in which all these things have their being."[7]

When I am sitting in meditation, therefore, I keep asking myself, "Who am I?" "What is my Source?" "Where is the Ground of my being?" And when any merely relative aspect of my life appears and suggests that it is I, I notice that I have taken a step back from it, toward my center, and I am looking at it neutrally. *It,* therefore, is not I; I, who am looking, am I.

We need a very alert consciousness to do this practice. We have to focus our consciousness inwardly, ever more and more inwardly and centrally, into the very heart and Source of our being. The partial aspects of being will try to break our con-centering and distract our attention to themselves. The Chinese meditation teachers call these distractions the thieves of the mind.[8] Jesus used this imagery too, saying: "But know this, that if the householder had known in what part of the night the thief was coming, he would have watched and would not have let his house be broken into" (Matthew 24:43).

Watching means staying awake. *Buddha* means being awake. Jesus says, "What I say to you, I say to all: Watch!" (Mark 13:37). Stay awake. Be Buddha. Don't let the thieves of your mind catch you napping and steal away your con-sciousness by deceiving you into believing that you are no more than some partial aspect of yourself.

Living inattentively is another form of doubt. Not giving full attention results from having a divided mind, only part of it is given to the matter at hand, whether it is work or meditation. Again, it is a question of giving ourselves with all our heart, mind, soul, and strength to whatever it is that we are doing at the moment. That is, doing it wholehearted-ly, whole-mindedly. When we can do that, root our whole heart, mind, soul, and strength in our God, our Source, our Center, our Ground, at the very core and most secret place in ourselves, then the Source, "who sees in secret, will reward us openly" (Matthew 6:6). That is to say, we will not only know who we really are, but we will be able to do whatever is at hand with skill and success.

A Japanese Zen practitioner tells a story of his student days when he engaged in intercollegiate fencing matches. When he thought out his strategy, he lost; when he acted intuitively without thinking, he won. He says that in the winning bouts, he "experienced moments I call the naked expression of enlightenment, in which I acted in response to my direct feeling and deepest mind, without considering victory or defeat, opponent or myself, and with no awareness of even engaging in a match . . . free from illusion or discrimination. . . . It is a matter of training oneself, through the principles of Zen, to act wholeheartedly in every circumstance."[9]

The story of St. Peter walking on the water points the same moral. When Peter first got out of the boat and began to walk on water, he was in a state of perfect concentration. His whole heart, soul, mind, and strength were fixed on Jesus, who was calling him, saying, "Come!" But he allowed the thieves of the mind to attack him. He noticed the wind and the waves—his imagination was distracted. He grew frightened—his emotions were distracted. Then he thought it was impossible for a man to walk on water—his intellect was distracted. He lost his resolution to continue—his will was distracted. He began to sink. Jesus, fortunately, caught him, but he reproached him: "O you of little faith, why did you doubt?" (Matthew 14:28–30).

Inattentiveness, not being wholehearted, is doubt, is not believing. Chogyam Trungpa says, "Whenever doubt arises, one should cut through it; doing that, one finds behind it a state of brilliant wakefulness. The doubt which must be cut through is not so much intellectual uncertainty, but general slothfulness"[10]

The same Japanese practitioner quoted above goes on to

say, "When we live inattentively we are apt to fall into partial discrimination. This is a state of mind in which egocentricity is fostered and human suffering enhanced. Therefore, whenever I become aware that I am relapsing, I remind myself that heaven and earth have the same root. Everything is One. . . . Nowadays, whatever I do, I am completely at one with it.[11]

All this can be summed up in the words of St. Paul: "Be watchful (wakeful, attentive), stand firm in your faith (do not doubt or divide your mind), be courageous (wholehearted), be strong (exert yourself to the utmost)" (1 Corinthians 16:13). It is necessary to put forth effort, to apply oneself strenuously. Paul uses the example of an athlete, and he urges that we also go into training as if we were going to compete in the Olympics. People discipline themselves severely for the sake of a "perishable wreath," he says, why can't we make at least an equal effort to seek so great a good as self-realization, the only good really worth having? Furthermore, it's no use merely talking about it. One may talk a good game, but doing is the only thing that counts (see 1 Corinthians 9:24–27). As Chogyam Trungpa says, "It is very soothing to talk about these things; however, if there is no exertion and wakefulness we are not even fingerpainting, but deceiving ourselves. . . . The practice tradition is the only hope."[12]

Jesus concluded his Sermon on the Mount with the warning that those who hear his words and *do* them will hold fast under storm, whereas those who hear but do not do, will fall (Matthew 7:24–27). Persevere in practice, he urges, and do not give up. Be like the man who importuned his neighbor for food to set before an unexpected guest (Luke 18:5–8). Be like the widow who relentlessly demanded from a judge a settlement in her case (Luke 18:1–5). Be like the shepherd who sought a lost sheep until he found it. Be like the woman who cleaned her whole house and searched everywhere to find the money she had lost (Luke 15:3–9). It will work.

> Ask and it will be given you; seek and you will find; knock, and it will be opened to you. For everyone who asks receives, and he who seeks finds, and to him who knocks it will be opened. (Luke 11:9–10)

This is, however, a costly and arduous enterprise. Jesus does not conceal this fact, and he advises people to think twice before they take it up. All familiar relations and habits must be forsaken; everything that we considered as constituting our life must be renounced. He's not taking any half-hearted disciples (see Luke 14:26–33). But "he who hates his life in this world will keep it for eternal life" (John 12:25; Mark 10:30). For "you will know the truth and the truth will make you free" (John 8:32).

If we are faithful in our practice, we will break through to our enlightenment, or, in the New Testament figure, the eschatological Son of Man will come. He comes suddenly, without warning, you don't know when. But when it happens, you'll know it. It will be like lightning that covers the whole sky from east to west (Matthew 24:27, 39, 42, 44).

It is interesting that many people who have had the enlightenment experience describe it in just such terms. Enlightenment is not merely a metaphor. According to reports, people actually have an experience in which their whole visual field is a pure brilliant light, or in which everything seems to turn into light, or is surrounded by an aureole of light.[13] One feels released or freed, as if let out of prison or returned home after being held hostage (redeemed), or as if "risen from the dead," according to the fourteenth-century Zen master Bassui.[14] Bassui also said, "The radiance of this Mind will light up every corner of a universe freed of every single blemish. You will be liberated at last from all entanglements. . . . The joy of this moment cannot be put into words."[15]

Yasutani Roshi (died 1973) has remarked, "The ecstasy is genuine enough, but your state of mind cannot be called natural until you have fully disabused yourself of the notion, 'I have become enlightened.' Mark this point well, for it is often misunderstood."[16] Phillip Kapleau explains: "The object . . . is the cultivation first of mindfulness and eventually mindlessness. These are two different degrees of absorption. Mindfulness is a state wherein one is totally aware in any situation and so always able to respond appropriately. Yet one is aware that he is aware. Mindlessness, on the other hand, or 'no-mindness' . . . , is a condition of such complete absorption that there is no vestige of self-awareness."[17]

Two effects arise from this realization. One is meritless work. The other is universal compassion. "All labor we entered into with such a mind is valued for itself, apart from what it may lead to. . . . Every act is an expression of the Buddha-mind."[18]

This is, of course, the nonattachment to the fruits of the work spoken of in the *Bhagavad-Gita*. In the New Testament it seems to be indicated in the simile of the servants who are not thanked for properly performing this service. We are told that we also, when we have done all that is commanded, should say, "We are unworthy servants; we have only done what was our duty" (Luke 17:10). Detachment from reward for action is also taught in the parable of the vineyard. Workers who have put in different amounts of time all receive the same wage (Matthew 20:1–16). Distinctions, divisions, comparisons have all disappeared.

Enlightenment is never for oneself alone but for the sake of all.[19] Jesus says, "For their sake I consecrate myself, that they also may be consecrated in truth" (John 17:19). Seeing others, one sees oneself. It is "imperative . . . to abandon the idea of a 'myself' standing in opposition to others," says Yasutani Roshi.[20] It will become quite natural and obvious to us to say "whatever you have done to the least of these my brethren, you have done it to me" (Matthew 25:40). Jesus describes himself as "the good shepherd. The good shepherd lays down his life for his sheep" (John 10:11). He comes "not to be served, but to serve, and to give his life as a ransom for many" (Matthew 20:28). This is echoed in the Bodhisattva vow: "Sentient beings are countless—I vow to save them all."[21]

The world is one interdependent Whole, and each one of us is that One Whole.[22] Each of us must realize with respect to every "other" that "I am in you and you are in me" (John 14:20), and that all together we constitute a single body: "We, though many, are one body in Christ, and individually members of one another" (Romans 12:5; cf. 1 Corinthians 12:12ff.). "If one member suffers, all suffer together; if one member is honored, all rejoice together" (1 Corinthians 12:26). This is why the Zen monk Shojun Bando says, "Unless everybody else attains Enlightenment, I cannot truly attain Enlightenment, so my destiny and everybody's destiny are one."[23]

Each of us who realizes this union of all must carry the sins of the world (John 1:29). The enlightened person, explains Morimoto Roshi, may have no problems of his own, "But there are many beings around him, and all these people still have all their own problems with them, and now all problems are his own. He is enlarged to cover everybody else, or everybody comes into his being. There is no distinction between his 'I' and the 'others.'"[24] One's practice at this point concerns how to utilize the characteristics of one's particular being so as to contribute to the salvation of all. This practice is endless.

The Enlightenment quest has now come full circle. We have con-centered ourselves by undivided attention to what we are doing, identified ourselves with the Ground of our being and not with our finite and particular expressions. We have become purified and unself-conscious instruments of the divine and realized our union with and presence in every being. This means that the infinite self, the Ground, is realized as perfectly present in every finite act.

"To realize the undifferentiated is a necessary first step," declares Yasutani Roshi. "But the realization is incomplete if it goes no further." It is a weak enlightenment if the formless ground is still seen as somehow separate, or other than, the world of particular forms.[25] It is the Ground *of* the forms and expresses itself in forms. "He is not the God of the dead but of the living" (Matthew 22:32) and must be seen as vividly present in each of them.

Thus, if one asks, "What is the true self?" we can answer, "I, who speak to you, am he" (John 4:26). "The world of discrimination and the world of undifferentiation are not two. . . . They are two aspects of the One.[26]

"I am in the Father, and the Father is in me." (John 14:10).

When the sun shines, its rays spread throughout the earth; when there is rain, the earth becomes wet.[27]

Be children of your Father in heaven: For he makes his sun rise on the evil and on the good, and sends rain on the just and unjust. . . . Be perfect, as your heavenly Father is perfect. (Matthew 5:45, 48).

Practice to become whole.

The Immaculate Conception, Our Original Face

T HE LADY who appeared to Bernadette Soubirous in the
grotto at Lourdes revealed herself in the words "I am the
Immaculate Conception." Bernadette reported this to the
local priest, who objected that the Lady should have said, "I
am the *fruit* of the Immaculate Conception." But Bernadette
insisted that the Lady had said, "I *am* the Immaculate
Conception."

One is reminded of Philip saying to Jesus, "Show us the
way," and Jesus replying, "I *am* the way." And again of
Martha saying, "I know that my brother will rise again on
the last day," and Jesus retorting, "I *am* the Resurrection." In
these two latter cases, the powerful utterance is contrasted
with the lesser meaning the central words might have had in
order to highlight the transhistorical significance of the
speaker. The usual way of using the word is pointedly rejected
as too external, too passive, too separate, and too temporal.

I think these stories are clues. They indicate that we are to
move to another level of understanding of these figures.
They are no longer to be looked on as singular human subjects who are produced by conception or who undergo resurrection. They are to be contemplated as the archetypes or
principles of these mysteries themselves.

The Lady who presented herself as the archetype of the

Immaculate Conception also gave another image. She instructed Bernadette to "wash in the spring and drink of it." There was no spring visible, but following the Lady's indication, Bernadette scratched the earth, and a trickle of water appeared. Minuscule at first, in the ensuing days and weeks it expanded to a full, flowing stream. In the more than one hundred years since 1858, pilgrims have flocked to the shrine, and many of them have bathed in the water and drunk it to the healing of their bodies and souls.

Is the free-flowing stream of healing and life, springing up from the earth in which it had lain hidden and unsuspected, also an archetype? Why not? Perhaps the Lady and the Spring together reveal the secret meaning of the Immaculate Conception.

The Spring shows that an archetype, though its power comes from its transhistorical significance, need not be unhistorical. There is real water at Lourdes, and real cures take place there. The Blessed Virgin Mary is a historical woman, but as the Immaculate Conception she *means* much more. The Lady and the Spring are a double icon of the purity and unity of the life hidden at the center of things, for us hitherto an unknown life, but one which when liberated and raised to consciousness is healing.

We have a number of icons, sacred images, and archetypes in our traditions that we can use or refer to in order to develop our own insights. Sometimes they may lend themselves to use in ways that go beyond what their official custodians anticipated. But these figures are common property of the universal culture, and it is their function to provoke vision in us; so we should give ourselves permission to relate to them in creative ways.

The tradition that protects the sacred history of the Blessed Virgin Mary holds that she and her son, Jesus, are special persons, set apart. They have qualities, virtues, powers that none of the rest of us could possibly have. Mary, for instance, is said to be our fallen race's solitary boast, for she alone of all her sex is sinless.

It is my contention that setting these figures apart in this way and denying that the rest of us can have the same qualities that they have make them religiously useless. If their most important features cannot be shared by us, we may admire them, even worship them, but we are not thereby enabled to attain the goal of our spiritual life. To attain this goal, we must find that we ourselves are free, complete, unified—that is, that we ourselves possess the adorable qualities of the great archetypes.

It is only when the great icons, the sacred persons who image the supreme values, are viewed as paradigms and revelations of what is actually true of all of us that they can exercise their spiritual power. They release that power precisely by revealing to us the secret of what we truly are, so that we may find that truth in ourselves.

It is in this way that I propose to treat the archetype of the Immaculate Conception. I hold that it is not a privilege reserved to one human being (or to four, in this tradition, counting Adam, Eve, and Jesus), but is a revelation of the truth about all of us. Our spiritual task is to discover that point in ourselves where *we are the Immaculate Conception.*

I further suggest that the archetype for the same truth in the Far East is our Original Face, the face we had before our parents were born. The Immaculate Conception stands for our original, true, unblemished nature, and so does the Original Face. It is my hope that looking at the Immaculate Conception with a little help from the commentators on the Original Face will enable us to have much deeper devotion to this beautiful icon and to put the power of the archetype to work revealing to us the truth about ourselves.

Many people confuse the Immaculate Conception with the Virgin Birth of Jesus. The Immaculate Conception refers to the beginning of Mary's own life, when she was conceived by her parents, Anne and Joachim. It does not comment on whether there was "sin" in the act of generation on the part of the parents but states that the new life so generated is not blemished. Immaculate Conception does not mean the conception of a child without sexual intercourse. "Sin" is not a euphemism for "sex."

The doctrine of the Immaculate Conception, although it was defined in the Roman Church quite recently, had had a long history prior to that event, having spread in the eastern part of the Roman Empire in the earliest times of Christianity (committed to writing in the *Protoevangelium of James* in the second century A.D.) and having been debated vigorously up through the Middle Ages. The dispute about Mary's sinlessness centered on when her exemption from the common condition took place, some saying at the Annunciation, others at some time during her prenatal life, and still others—the Immaculists, who ultimately triumphed—at her conception. The main problem, that Christ is the Redeemer of *all* human beings who must be at some point in their lives sinners in need of redemption, was overcome by the idea of Original Grace, suggested by St. Maxim of Turin in the fifth century. This notion was taken up by Duns Scotus in 1300 and developed to mean that Mary was redeemed by the merits of Christ, body and soul, from the first moment of her life. The final formulation of the doctrine in the West appeared in the Apostolic Constitution *Ineffabilis Deus,* issued by Pope Pius IX on December 8, 1854, and states:

> We declare, pronounce, and define that the most Blessed Virgin Mary, in the first instant of her Conception, by a singular grace and privilege granted by Almighty God, in view of the merits of Jesus Christ, the Savior of the human race, was preserved free from all stain of original sin, is a doctrine revealed by God and therefore to be believed firmly and constantly by all the faithful.

It is the teaching of the Church that this is a special privilege for Mary alone, does not apply to the rest of humanity, and does not derive from her nature but from a special grace granted her by God. I repeat this in order to be clear, for I am going to interpret this doctrine in a way that will both negate this exclusivity and give it a new meaning.

The dogma of the Immaculate Conception, therefore, says that the Blessed Virgin Mary, in view of the fact that she was destined to become the mother of Christ, was preserved at the beginning of her life from the stain of Original Sin. She was created clean, she was conceived immaculate. She was always in that state which the rest of us attain by baptism, the state of grace. In other words, she was created and "saved" simultaneously. This is the fundamental theological significance of this dogma.

To begin to appreciate what this can mean, what it is to be immaculate, we need to inquire about the *macula* from which she was preserved. This "spot," or stain, or taint, or blight, or blemish, or injury, or distortion, or deformity, is Original Sin. But what is that? It is not so much the first sin (though it is that too)—not "original" in that sense—as the sin that is somehow already present even when we originate, which surrounds us from our very origin:

O see, in guilt I was born,
A sinner was I conceived. (Psalm 51:5)

The doctrine expresses our experience that we get started with at least two strikes against us. We are born into a situation, a world, that is already warped and diseased before we even have an opportunity to add our own twists and injuries to it. Paraphrasing, we may say:

I was wounded by iniquity from the moment of my birth; indeed, I was trapped in sin from my very conception.

Original Sin is said to be hereditary. How can that be? How can I be blamed for something someone else did? But it's not sin in that sense. It's not something someone did. Or rather, it's something that everyone does. And strictly speaking, it's not something that anyone is "blamed" for, although we are all "punished" for it—or by it. It is the condition of hurt, of distortion, of impeded life. And it is hereditary in this sense: because our parents and other community members have been hurt in their time and learned selfish and hurting ways of coping and trying to protect themselves, they put us in a situation in which we are obliged to adapt to them and to the world they have made by engineering our own hurtful responses. It is this "chain reaction" that is pointed to by the doctrine of the "inheritance" of Original Sin.

Sin is usually said to be separation from God. I shall say that this means separation from free-flowing, spontaneous, self-sharing, immortal life. (This way of putting it will help us to make connections with the Buddhist insights later on.) This life is unself-conscious. It doesn't double itself. It doesn't watch itself living and judge itself (or others). This is why it does not have any impediment but can be free-flowing and spontaneous. It is a fundamental unity:

Hear, O Israel, the Lord your God, the Lord is One.

Sin is any impediment to this unity, any "spot" that divides the unbroken field into two, that sets up polarity and opposition.

Everything that we popularly call "sin," and all the psychological roots from which these behaviors derive, is based on alienation, on *other*ness, on division, on separation, on estrangement. Original Sin is the ground and foundation for all the particular sins which we actually commit, the fundamental sense of alienation, the impediment to the free flow of spontaneous life. Immaculate Conception, therefore, means freedom from this impediment, from alienation and self-division.

There is also a story about Original Sin in the sense of its being the "first" sin, the root of all the rest, and this story points to the same truth, that all sin takes its rise from duality and self-consciousness. The story depicts the first sin as consisting of eating the fruit of the Tree of Knowledge of Good and Evil, and afterward realizing nakedness and shame. The earlier consciousness of simple unity has been broken up. Experience is now had in the mode of duality, by pairs of opposites, through the sense of contrast. Things are compared, distinguished, separated, preferred. By such means it is thought that their identity is established and that they are *known*. And most important, they are judged as being either "good" or "evil." But good or evil with respect to what? With respect to *me*. The self has become self-conscious, and everything is now referred to *me* for meaning and value. Everything *known* by me is something *else*, something not-self. I am suddenly separate from the rest of the world. I am opposite to them (the known) and they are opposite to me (the knower and the judge). I am no longer simply flowing freely and spontaneously in unity with them, I am not sharing myself with them. My self is apart; they are others to me. I hold myself away from them; I hide myself from them. I am not willing to be naked before them and with them. I am ashamed and must protect myself.

The final consequence of this self-consciousness and knowledge of everything in terms of its being good or evil for me is that I must struggle and suffer to try to maintain my life in the world, and in the end I die. When I identify only with my limited self—the self who "knows" the "others" and knows itself as knowing that it knows, and is separated by this knowledge—when I so identify, I remove myself from the harmonious, free-flowing, spontaneous stream of immortal life. I have identified with something limited that must die, and so "I" will die. And in the meantime I try to protect myself by wresting my life from the lives of the "others," setting myself against every other being. I perceive them as against me and I feed myself only with sweat and labor, and what life I succeed in producing I give birth to with pain.

The great myths, the sacred stories, always tell about beginning, about roots. To tell about the creation of something is to tell about its basic nature. The examination of fundamentals is cast in the idiom of beginnings. And the way things *are* is frequently described as due to something someone *did*. It may not be a "once done" something, but a continually done something, something we are still doing.

But to tell about it as if it took its rise from some act com-

mitted at the dawn of existence is to say that this is a fundamental characteristic of our life and has always been with us.
To represent it as something the original actor need not have
done is to say that it is not absolutely necessary, though
probably emotionally or developmentally almost inevitable.
To dramatize it as disobedience to God is to say that fundamental and inevitable though it may be, we realize in some
part of our being that it is not really in our best interest, not
the ideal condition for us, indeed enormously harmful to us.
And to recite the whole story as myth, as sacred lore, is to
acknowledge that we are profoundly puzzled by the situation, which appears to us paradoxical: something so basic in
us, yet not to our good.

It is against this background that the Immaculate Conception says that there is something yet more fundamental,
which is the unimpaired unity, still present and available. It
is this unity that is expressed by the mythic figure of the
Immaculata, the one who is sinless from the beginning. She
is not engaged in duallty. She has the "single eye" and consequently is "full of light" and "full of grace."

The mysteries—the secrets of human nature and destiny—
have always been told as if they were only external events.
And indeed many of them were embodied in external events
in historical time. When they appear in sacred lore, they have
no doubt been edited and expanded in order to express the
religious experience of the community that created that liter-
ature (oral or written), but they had a foundation in fact.

This mode of presentation makes the mysteries easily
accessible to everyone, whatever degree of mental subtlety
one is able to muster. It also keeps the note of concrete reality,
so important when dealing with the invisible and the intan-
gible, so that there is no confusion with abstraction. It pro-
vides material for liturgy and community celebration,
appropriate elements in the quest for enlightenment about
human nature and destiny, since the human being is essentially communitarian.

The stories and the heroic figures provide idealized models for individuals in their self-shaping efforts that are part of the quest. And best of all, the same stories and emblems can be read at various levels, reread in each stage of our development, revealing gradually the deeper layers of meaning that they contain. As one progresses in understanding, the mythic events (including basically historical happenings that carry the meanings of the mysteries) show themselves as more and more universal and therefore paradigms of the essential experience of everyone.

It is one of the unrecognized poverties of the affluent age that so many of us are unable to live with and work with and learn from our sacred lore in this way. The modern one-dimensional mind, weaned on scientific fact and newspaper reporting, takes only the simplistic external interpretation, cares only for the putative historical happening, and either neglects or rejects the universal application of the mystery so presented. This shallow mindedness prevents the great tradition from fulfilling its sacred function, that of gradually and developmentally unfolding to us the secrets of who and what we really are.

Perhaps it is in order to avoid this misunderstanding that the mythic figures occasionally interrupt the historical-time sequence of their story to declare that they represent or embody some eternal truth. When the archetype announces that it is the Way, or the Resurrection, or the Immaculate Conception, it is identifying itself clearly, fairly, and unambiguously, lest we mistake it for something more limited and individual and less universal than it really is.

Another remark that is perhaps worth making is that the traditional archetypes are available to everyone. You don't have to be a Christian to take the Immaculate Conception to heart as a significant revelation to you personally; nor do you have to be a Buddhist to realize that the emblem of the Original Face was meant for you. Once these highly charged symbols enter the mainstream of human culture, they belong to all of us, and we need not be shy about adopting them as our own.

What I am saying, then, is that this mystery emblem, the Immaculate Conception, is about *us*. It may be also true in the limited and particular sense taught by its official custodians, but my point is that as an archetype it is about *our* true selfhood, *our* consciousness, *our* reality. The view I am proposing regards the whole sacred story, including all its characters, as played out within ourselves by the various aspects of our humanness and our personhood. Taking it this way, we can give a new meaning even to the "exclusive" elements of official dogma.

Our "Mary" aspect is that part of us represented by the icon of the Blessed Virgin Mary. To say that it *alone* has the privilege of Immaculate Conception is to say that only this central Mary principle in us is free from Original Sin. Obviously, most, if not all, other aspects of us are contaminated. After all, it was the overwhelming fact that human nature is engulfed in wickedness (even, bafflingly, against its will) that set off the quest for enlightenment and purification in the first place. That there should be at least *one* point in us that *is* free is a great discovery, something to be carefully taught in the sacred mysteries by emphasizing its singularity and uniqueness.

Further, this Immaculate Conception aspect of ourselves is free from sin not by virtue of the nature of humanity (considered as a biological species), which is derived by evolution from the fundamental constituents of the physical universe and built up in large part by the selfish practices necessary to accomplish the task. But the Immaculate Conception in us is the presence in us of the "grace of God," the sharing of divine life, something that quite transcends the principles on which the natural universe operates. It is the presence of *personhood* in us, something that cannot be reduced to the motions of molecules. Personhood is what makes us all incomparably valuable, what gives us transcendent dignity and therefore makes us equal. Our particular qualities of genetic endowment and individual development may make differences among us, but when we focus on our right to equal respect, we are speaking of ourselves as persons.[1]

By such interpretations we can accommodate the traditional claims for the singularity and supernatural privilege of the Immaculate Conception, and in the process say something which, even from the extratraditional point of view, we consider valid and vital. Nevertheless, I hold that this mysterious grace-filled aspect is to be found in everyone, no matter how deeply buried, obscured, and overladen with "sin," and that we have each had it from the beginning of our lives.

In fact, I would suggest that it is our "beginning," the point from which we start, our "point of departure." Thomas Merton speaks of something he calls "the virgin point between darkness and light, between nonbeing and being."[2]

> At the center of our being is a point of nothingness which is untouched by sin and by illusion, a point of pure truth, a point or spark which belongs entirely to God, which is never at our disposal, from which God disposes of our lives, which is inaccessible to the fantasies of our own mind or the brutality of our own will. . . . It is in everybody and if we could see it . . . that would make all the darkness and cruelty of life vanish completely. . . . I have no program for this seeing. It is only given. But the gate of heaven is everywhere.[3]

Madeline Abdelnour, in her article "*Le Point Vierge* in Thomas Merton," cites various authors in the mystical tradition of the West who have spoken of something similar, some "central point of the soul" that is the locus of the human union with the divine. Most of these writers struggled with the task of holding the two realms in contact without committing themselves to a monistic position: "In this struggle to describe this 'spark of the soul,' it is at one moment presented as the divine to which the self attains; at another, as that transcendent aspect of the self united with God."[4]

This suggests to my mind the rather abstract notion of *interface* and the more concrete image of the *umbilicus*, the source of inflowing life, the join of parent and child. Could this be (part of) the meaning of the Immaculate Conception? The central point of our being that is an interface with what transcends the finite boundaries of our humanity and yet is our own truest self? Perhaps we should give serious attention to the idea of contemplating our navel, memento and symbol of that mysterious connection which is our beginning.

The Immaculate Conception, the unflawed Beginning, still present and functioning in every one of us, is our own private, yet shared, Paradise. As Barbara Myerhoff says, "All paradise myths"—and the Immaculate Conception is a kind of paradise myth—symbolize "the state which existed before the world began."[5]

The Buddhists say, our Original Face existed before our parents were born. But this "bliss is lost at the moment of primordial splitting, after which nothing can be the same," says Myerhoff. Primordial splitting is the introduction of the *macula*, the "spot" that interrupts original unity.

And yet, Original Unity remains. It is an eternal truth. It cannot cease to exist. We have only lost sight of it. Because we have lost sight of this truth, the icon appears initially to be something other than ourselves. We project it. We need to remind ourselves that the icons arise in *our consciousness*, thus testifying to their reality in *us*. We would not think these things—the great mythic archetypes—if they were not true of us and in us. Thus we have *recourse* to the archetype, we "run back" to it, in order to come again to our paradisiac selfhood. And this archetype of the Immaculate Conception acts as an interface, as an *intercessor*. . . . "O Mary, conceived without sin, pray for us who have recourse to thee" is the mantram of the Immaculate Conception.

Somewhere in us, says my thesis, is the reality that the archetypal, mythical image of Immaculate Conception represents: somewhere at the center of our being, at the interface between our human being proper and the transcendent Source from which that derives, at our spiritual navel, where existence is originally communicated to us. It is a singular and special point, untouched by "sin" (Western term) or "illusion" (Eastern term), not subject to the biological programs of human nature; it is the source in us of that unselfconscious, spontaneous, free-flowing Original Life that we call divine. Losing touch with that flow has meant our expulsion from "Paradise," a kind of forgetting of the truth about ourselves, of who we really are. And yet who-we-really-are is still there; we still have our original face.

A famous Zen koan is "Show me your original face, the face you had before your parents were born." Understood rationally, and assuming that the "face" referred to is the face that develops in the course of the life that the parents have engendered, there is no solution to this riddle. Nevertheless, it is one of the "gates of heaven." The Zen master does not expect the disciple to give an explanation of the puzzle. The master hopes that the disciple will come in some day actually displaying this original face.

Suppose we try to find our original face by meditatively retracing our lifeline back through the years of our maturity, through our youth and childhood, through our prenatal gestation, to our conception.[6] What happens to all the descriptive qualities by which we identify and situate ourselves? Are they not one after another stripped off? When we are no more than a tiny blob of protoplasm, who and what are "we"? And if each of us retires, in this backward journey, into the body of that parent of ours that produced it, and if these, our parents, retract to the eggs and sperms from which *they* were formed, what do we mean by "we" then? What "face" do "we" have at that point, before our parents themselves were born?

Such an imaginative journey may help to shake us loose from our steadfast presuppositions, from the "obvious" realities in which we have always believed. Any way that we had of thinking of "ourselves" that was connected with the particular body we have at present has to be lost in the process of performing this meditation. Every time we repeat the meditation, we eliminate more and more subtle characteristics. We find that the categories into which we sort our perceptions of the world are programs of our brains. The traits of our personalities are attached to the histories (genetic and developmental) of our bodies. Everything about us that can be considered "sin" or "illusion" is a compound of such traits and categories and their derived and conditioned behaviors, and therefore has to be abandoned. If there is any "self" left at all, it is a pure point of existence, an absolutely empty mirror, having no qualities of its own.

And then the breakthrough may happen. We may suddenly realize that just because this mirror is absolutely empty, it can reflect faithfully all that is shown it. Because it has no interruptions, it is like a smooth continuous flow. Because it does not manipulate itself, it is simple and spontaneous. Because it is not temporal, it must be eternal. (So the whole imaginative exercise by which we provoke the breakthrough, this retracing in time, is inapplicable.) And finally, if this is true of us, then it must be true of everyone. Or, better, since this real being is empty, it cannot be cut off from any being by contrast of qualities; and since it is a continuous flow of life, it cannot be broken up into separate compartments by defining barriers. Consequently, those sorrows and sufferings that are due to the perception of contrast, possession of qualities, separation, isolation, inhibition of the free flow of spontaneous life—all these disappear. Bliss floods the consciousness, and the disciple returns to the master with the Original Face shining in every glance and gesture.

This is the hoped for realization. Those who experience it say such things as:

I have seen my Face before my parents were born clearer than a diamond in the palm of my hand.[7]

I surely had seen the root of nothingness; after three years of practice I saw my original face.[8]

[I comprehend nothingness and at the same time] the true form of Kannon [or Kwan Yin, feminine icon of the Buddhist ideal] and the true form of myself, indeed the true form of all things. All is one. Whatever one may say, there can be no denying it. What I attained was seeing through to the original self.[9]

In fact, all koans point to our "Face before our parents were born," that is, to our real self. It is the covering designation for all questions such as "What am I?" "Where did I come from?" "What is my meaning, my destiny?"[10] And the answer comes out, effectively, "I am the Immaculate Conception."

Immaculate is a recurring word in Buddhist efforts to convey their realization. For instance, in Dom Aelred Graham's *Conversations Christian and Buddhist,* the Reverend Kobori Sohaku says:

K.S. Buddhism is a religion which teaches that a human being is originally Buddha, originally immaculate, originally complete in nature.
A.G. The original face.
K.S. The original face is covered. So we human beings should wipe off this cloud, this stain.[11]

The famous fourteenth-century Rinzai Zen master Bassui said:

One's whole being is Buddha-nature. One's whole being is the Great Way [Mahayana]. The substance of this Way is inherently immaculate and transcends all forms. Man's own Mind is the essential substance of all Buddhas, his Face before his parents' birth.[12]

and again, in his Sermon on One-Mind:

This mind is intrinsically pure. . . . It has no distinction of male or female, nor has it any coloration of good or bad. It cannot be compared with anything, so it is called Buddha-nature.[13]

And:

> The Mind-essence is intrinsically bright and unblemished.[14]

It is not only the Japanese tradition that speaks in this way. John Blofeld reports that a Tibetan Buddhist mantram says, "Spotlessly pure are all dharmas [constituents of reality] and spotlessly pure am I!"[15] And the contemporary American roshi Philip Kapleau teaches that the movement from ignorance to awareness of truth "implies the emergence into the field of consciousness of the immaculate Bodhi-mind."[16]

This immaculate, spotless, nature is said to be our real self, obscured and hidden from us by our delusions and our ignorance. In this respect it is like the spring at Lourdes, hidden underground, awaiting its uncovering. It was there all the time, but it had to be released. Similarly, Dōgenzenji (Japanese, thirteenth century) teaches that we are ontologically Buddha-nature, whether we know it or not:

> It is the non-believers who steadfastly maintain that Buddha-nature is there or not there depending on consciousness or non-consciousness, that it is nature or not-nature depending on knowledge or non-knowledge. For a long time unknowing ones have taken the activity of consciousness for Buddha-nature and the original face.[17]

According to T'ien-ju Wei-tse, a great figure in Chinese Buddhism in the fourteenth century, "You are each in possession of 'the original face' which is the same as it is in all the Buddhas, only that in us it is not recognized."[18] Bassui agrees:

> This Mind . . . called one's Face before one's parents were born . . . is the true nature of sentient beings, that which presently exists unchanged and eternal. . . . This Mind is latent in everyone. . . . But its clarity is hidden by delusive thoughts just as . . . the moon is obscured by clouds. Yet such thoughts can be dispelled. . . . Once they vanish, the Buddha-nature reveals itself. . . . This light has ever been present: it is not newly obtained outside yourself.[19]

When enlightenment comes, says twentieth-century Yasutani-roshi, "it is the sudden realization that 'I have been complete and perfect from the beginning. How wonderful, how miraculous!'"[20] As Thomas Merton says, "Here is an unspeakable secret: paradise is all around us and we do not understand."[21]

"Paradise," of course, means the same thing as the Immaculate Conception: the reality prior to (or without) sin and suffering. If the myth of Paradise and the loss of Paradise is joined to those other images, we may catch a glimpse of what the *macula* itself basically is. I suggested earlier that it is knowing by comparing things (measuring) and especially by judging them as good or evil. This implies the dualism of subject and object and the separation of the knower and everything else. D. T. Suzuki tells us that "ordinarily, we go out of ourselves to seek a place of ultimate rest" in a different-from-self Deity and at a time in the future. But:

> Zen takes the opposite course and steps backwards . . . to reach . . . a point before the world with all its dichotomies has yet made its debut . . . a world in which time and space have not yet put their cleaving wedges. . . . Buddhists want us to see our own "original face" even before we were born . . . to be with God even before he commanded light to be . . . where there is as yet no subject to assert itself, no object to be taken hold of: where there is neither seer nor the seen.[22]

Is this what the Immaculate Conception means? A state of mind prior to knowing according to good and evil, even prior to the bifurcation into subject and object? A purity of reality and consciousness that is (necessarily) present in all of us as the very foundation of all divisive forms of consciousness? It is my suggestion that this is its significance as an archetype. And when enlightenment comes, we find that this ground of purity, this Immaculate Conception, in us has become "the Woman clothed with the Sun," clothed in radiance and generosity. This is another title of the Blessed Virgin

Mary and therefore another image of our reality. To be clothed with the sun is to express oneself in unremitting giving, to be a constant output of energy that passes away.

In the lineage of history, the Immaculate Conception meant a break in the chain of sin, of deception and bondage. It meant a new beginning, a fresh start. Translated into a process context in which it stands for something that *goes on continuously*, it means what Joseph Campbell calls "a continuous shattering of the crystallizations of the moment."[23] Any crystallization is a bondage. To believe in it is deception.

But the Zen Mind, the Original Face Mind, is a beginner's mind; that is, it is fresh each instant, meeting the new reality of the present moment without prejudice. Shunryu Suzuki says, in *Zen Mind, Beginner's Mind*, "The goal of practice is always to keep our beginner's mind . . . always ready for anything, it is open to everything. In the beginner's mind, there are many possibilities; in the expert's mind there are few."[24]

The Original Face, the Immaculate Conception, is able to be free of prejudice, preconception, crystallization, because it has a certain quality of *emptiness*. Sometimes emptiness is attributed to female images and is interpreted as an emptiness that will be filled by the male god. That is not what is meant here. This is an emptiness that is characteristic of the Absolute itself. It means transcendence of all form, of all particularity. Mystics sometimes call it "the desert." Thomas Merton, speaking of it, says: "Emptiness. Total poverty of the Creator: yet from this poverty springs everything."[25]

This is just the point: from this poverty or emptiness springs everything. This is why the Immaculate Conception is also the Woman who shines as the sun, who is effulgence and free-flowing energy. That which is nothing in particular is the source of everything. Not determined by another, it is spontaneous. Uninhibited by extraneous values, it is unselfconscious. And this is our natural mind, our Original Face.

The original sin was objectivizing everything, especially ourselves, so that we judged everything, including ourselves. This habit of judging—knowing as good or evil—made us self-conscious and inhibited, hence simultaneously shy, defensive, and aggressive. Our life became blocked and distorted. The Immaculate Conception represents the return to what we originally are, to the purity, or plainness, of consciousness of the world without complications. But the world can be seen clearly, in its own terms, only by a mind that is not warped and distracted by attention to concepts of itself and things in relation to itself. An immaculate mind, free of these impediments, transcendent of all descriptions that might be extraneously laid on it, an *empty* mind, like a clean mirror, can then perceive the world as it is in itself.

And what the immaculate mind sees is the Buddha-nature of everything, beyond the distortions and the overlays of deception and sin. The immaculate mind sees everything connected, everything radiant, clothed with the sun. This is what is called—for good reason—Illumination or Enlightenment. Everything is seen to be of the nature of light, in the sense that it is essentially transcendent of particular form, though also expressing in form, and in the sense that it is free-flowing and spontaneous in its continuous process activity, and in the sense that it is radiant in giving itself away and sharing its being with all.

In Dōgen's view,

All reality, as Buddha-nature, is one. The way [to realization] requires the constant step beyond into the formless, the indeterminate. . . . But nothingness is not a point of rest attained. Only by realizing the dynamism of reality in becoming is Buddha-nature fully unfolded.[26]

And James Conner, writing of "The Original Face in Buddhism and the True Self in Thomas Merton," says:

The fully enlightened mind, the fully emptied person, contains the universe in its totality perfectly. It is characterized by an all-embracingness that knows no bounds. . . . It is able to accept all . . . without preference or prejudice. It reflects each . . . in its uniqueness and values each as such. And it is able to respond to each in the manner that is appropriate in every circumstance. Such a universal availability . . . is only possible to the fully emptied person . . . without taint.[27]

This untainted consciousness, the Immaculate Conception, our Original Face, like Thomas Merton's *point vierge*, "is in everybody, and if we could see it, we would see those billions of points of light coming together in the face and blaze of the sun that would make all the darkness and cruelty of life vanish completely."[28]

And indeed, Gautama Buddha himself is reported to have exclaimed at his Enlightenment, "Wonder of wonders! Intrinsically all living beings are Buddhas, endowed with wisdom and virtue, but because men's minds have become inverted through delusive thinking, they fail to perceive this."[29]

Perhaps there is some strange significance in the fact that this marvelous event, the Buddha's Enlightenment, is supposed to have occurred on December 8, the date chosen for the celebration of the Feast of the Immaculate Conception. Perhaps the secret meaning of the Immaculate Conception is that there is a point in each of us that is free from sin from the beginning, endowed with wisdom and virtue, but—like the underground spring of healing at Lourdes—it has been hidden from us by delusive thinking. If so, then the Blessed Virgin Mary, as the archetype of this secret sinless self, may be understood as revealing our true nature to us and thus guiding us to its discovery.

Notes

Chapter 1: Religion Is Experience

1. This story appears also in *Living Prayer* (July/August, 1995).

2. Another example of this, I believe, is the conversation with Nicodemus, which, by contrast, takes place "by night," indicating a different stage or aspect of the journey. See my "Nicodemus by Night," *Sisters Today* 67/1 (Jan., 1995).

3. He himself had tried—and discarded—a number of things he might have given himself to, a number of conclusions to the hypothesis "*If* you are the Son of God, *then* . . ." (Matthew 4:3ff.).

4. Cf. Diotima's lesson on love to Socrates, *Symposium* 210–212: begin with love of beautiful individuals, but move on to beautiful institutions and beautiful ideas.

5. Consult A. Reza Arasteh, *Final Integration in the Adult Personality* (Leiden: Brill, 1965), who develops the theme of transcultural consciousness. Also, David Riesman, *The Lonely Crowd* (New Haven: Yale University Press, 1950), speaks of "those whom I call autonomous . . . people capable of transcending their culture" (p. 290). See Arasteh (pp. 212–217) for a number of interesting parallels to our story in the story of Rumi and Shams.

6. In the chakra schema, the ascending Shakti, the drive to be more, imaged as female, is united to the unmoving, unlimited Being, Shiva, imaged as male, at the crown of the human being, the seventh chakra. This union is the Total Reality.

7. Cf. Bruno Barnhart, *The Good Wine: Reading John from the Center* (New York: Paulist, 1993). pp. 84–85, "last day" as Sabbath; p. 111, the "one work" of the "*new union of humanity with God,*" which "*work is itself the great sabbath*" which was "made for humanity" and will be realized once Jesus has made humanity "equal with God." Cf. pp. 114–15: The man born blind, whose eyes are opened by Jesus, identifies himself saying, "*I am*" (John 9:9).

Chapter 2: The Ways of Realization

1. This exercise is further spelled out in my upcoming book, *The Easter Mysteries,* to be published by Crossroad in 1995.

Chapter 3: The Search for the Self

1. Surendranath Dasgupta, *Hindu Mysticism* (New York: Ungar, 1927), pp. 65–66, 69.

2. Swami Abhishiktananda, *The Further Shore* (Delhi: I.S.P.C.K., 1975), pp. 26, 27.

3. Arthur Osborne, *Ramana Marshi and the Path of Self-Knowledge* (New York: Samuel Weiser Inc., 1954), p. 23.

4. Swami Abhishiktananda, *The Secret of Arunachala* (Delhi: I.S.P.C.K., 1979), p. 82.

5. Ibid., p. 83.

Chapter 4: The Mystery of Nondualism

1. Sri Aurobindo Ghose, "Liberation," *Last Poems* (Cento: Nontanari, 1972).

2. Master Rinzai, Discourse XVII; Eido Tai Shimano, *Points of Departure* (New York: Zen Studies Society Press, 1991), p. 85.

3. See John 1:12: to all who "believed in" him, "he gave *exousia* to become children of God." *Exousia* can be translated "the right," or "authority," but it means literally "out of one's own being." The verse goes on to say of these believers that they "*were* born . . . of God." If they had already been "born of God," perhaps we could read: "He acknowledged them as being children of God."

4. Eido Tai Shimano, *Points of Departure*, pp. 27, 30.

5. Ibid., pp. 85, 12, 7.

6. Ibid., p. 33.

7. Ibid., pp. 15, 9, 121, 122.

8. Ibid., p. 11.

9. Ibid., pp. 106, 179.

10. Master Han Shan, *Autobiography*, cited without further reference in Garma C. C. Chang, *The Buddhist Teaching of Totality* (University Park and London: Pennsylvania State University Press, 1971), p. 178.

11. Master Hsüeh Yen, *Autobiography*, Garma C. C. Chang, *Buddhist Teaching*, p. 179.

Chapter 5: Enlightenment and Practice

1. Katsuki Sekida, *Zen Training* (New York: Weatherhill, 1975), pp. 237ff.

2. Garma C. C. Chang, *The Buddhist Teaching of Totality* (University Park and London: Pennsylvania State University Press, 1971).

3. Hee-jin Kim, *Dōgen Kigen: Mystical Realist* (Tucson: University of Arizona Press, 1975), pp. 66.

4. Kim, *Dōgen Kigen*, p. 122.

5. Ibid., p. 61.

6. Ibid., p. 193.

7. Ibid., p. 83.

8. Eido Tai Shimano, *Points of Departure* (New York: Zen Studies Society Press, 1991), p. 152.

9. Swami Abhishiktananda, *The Further Shore* (Delhi: I.S.P.C.K., 1975), p. 56.

Chapter 6: Gospel Zen

1. Roshi Philip Kapleau, *The Three Pillars of Zen* (Boston: Beacon Press, 1967), pp. 331, 347, 330. (N.B. Pagination is different in new expanded edition of 1980; e.g., p. 96 of 1967 edition = p. 103 of 1980 edition.)

2. Achaan Chah, *A Still Forest Pool* (Wheaton, IL: Quest, 1985), p. 30.

3. J. Z. Young, *Programs of the Brain* (New York: Oxford, 1978), p. 15.

4. Ibid., 12ff.

5. Heinz R. Pagels, *Perfect Symmetry* (New York: Simon and Schuster, 1985), pp. 200ff.; Erich Jantsch, *The Self-Organizing Universe* (New York: Pergamon, 1980), p. 222ff.

6. Kapleau, *Three Pillars*, 311; cf. James 1:18, 27.

7. Robert Powell, *The Blissful Life* (Durham, NC: Acorn, 1884), p. 7.

8. Dom Aelred Graham, *Conversations: Christian and Buddhist* (New York: Harcourt, Brace, and World, 1968), p. 66.

9. Kapleau, *Three Pillars*, p. 232.

10. Hakuyu Taizan Maezumi, and Bernard Tetsugen Glassman, *The Hazy Moon of Enlightenment* (Los Angeles: Center Publications, 1978), p. viii.

11. Kapleau, *Three Pillars*, p. 232.

12. Maezumi and Glassman, *The Hazy Moon*, p. viii.

13. J. M. Cohen, and J. F. Phipps, *The Common Experience* (Los Angeles: Tarcher, 1979), p. 141ff.; Roshi Jiyu Kennett, *The Wild White Goose*, vol. 1 (Mt. Shasta, CA: Shasta Abbey, 1977), p. 68.

14. Kapleau, *Three Pillars*, p. 182.

15. Ibid., p. 169.

16. Ibid., p. 56.

17. Ibid., pp. 200–201.

18. Ibid., p. 201.

19. Ibid.

20. Ibid., p. 106.

21. Ibid., p. 201.

22. Ibid., p. 64.

23. Graham, *Conversations*, p. 167.

24. Ibid., p. 45.

25. Kapleau, *Three Pillars*, pp. 120, 286n.

26. Ibid., p. 120.

27. Ibid., p. 116.

Chapter 7: Immaculate Conception

1. The distinction between human nature and person is discussed at length in B. Bruteau, "Trinitarian Personhood," *Cistercian Studies* 22/3 (1987), 199–212. An expanded meaning and application of the term "grace" is also developed here.

2. Thomas Merton, *Conjectures of a Guilty Bystander* (Garden City, NY: Doubleday Image, 1968), p. 132.

3. Ibid., p. 158.

4. Sister M. Madeline Abdelnour, S.C.N., "*Le Point Vierge* in Thomas Merton," *Cistercian Studies* 6/2 (1971), p. 156.

5. Barbara Myerhoff, "Balancing between Worlds: The Shaman's Calling," *Parabola* 1:2 (Spring, 1976), Myth and Quest for Meaning, p. 12.

6. Cf. William Johnston, *The Mirror Mind* (New York: Harper & Row, 1981), p. 37.

7. Roshi Philip Kapleau, *The Three Pillars of Zen* (revised and expanded edition; Garden City, NY: Anchor Doubleday, 1980), p. 290.

8. Heinrich Dumoulin, *Zen Enlightenment*, tr. John C. Maraldo (New York: Weatherhill, 1979), p. 150.

9. Ibid.

10. Kapleau, *Three Pillars*, p. 70.

11. Dom Aelred Graham, *Conversations: Christian and Buddhist* (New York: Harcourt, Brace, and World, 1968), p. 37.

12. Kapleau, *Three Pillars*, pp. 172–73.

13. Ibid., p. 170.

14. Ibid., p. 176.

15. John Blofeld, *The Tantric Mysticism of Tibet* (New York: Causeway, 1974), p. 174.

16. Kapleau, *Three Pillars*, p. 72; cf. "our immaculate Bodhi-mind shines brightly," p. 21.

17. Dumoulin, *Zen Enlightenment*, p. 121.

18. Tien-ju Wei-tse, *Sayings*, vol. II, cited in Daisetz Teitaro Suzuki, *Essays in Zen Buddhism*, Second Series, ed. Christmas Humphreys (New York: Weiser, 1971), p. 150.

19. Kapleau, *Three Pillars*, pp. 169, 176.

20. Ibid., p. 50.

21. Merton, *Conjectures*, p. 132.

22. D. T. Suzuki, *Living by Zen*, ed. Christmas Humphreys (London: Rider, 1972), pp. 70–71.

23. Joseph Campbell, *The Hero with a Thousand Faces* (Bollingen Series XVII; Princeton: Princeton University Press, 1973), p. 337.

24. Shunryu Suzuki, *Zen Mind, Beginner's Mind* (New York: Weatherhill, 1977), p. 21.

25. Thomas Merton, *Familiar Liturgies of Misunderstanding* (New York: New Directions, 1967), p. 58.

26. Dumoulin, *Zen Enlightenment*, p. 121.

27. James Conner, "The Original Face in Buddhism and the True Self in Thomas Merton," *Cistercian Studies* 22/4 (1987), p. 345.

28. Merton, *Conjectures*, p. 142.

29. Kapleau, *Three Pillars*, p. 31.